dare to believe

A GUIDE TO USING YOUR FAITH WITHOUT LIMITS

EVELYN McCOY

Please note that certain pronouns in Scripture that refer to the Father, Son, and Holy Spirit are capitalized and may differ from some publishers' styles.
Scripture taken from King James Version, Public Domain. Used by permission.

Copyright © 2012 Evelyn McCoy
All rights reserved.
ISBN: 147015918X
ISBN-13: 9781470159184
Library of Congress Control Number: 2012904207

CreateSpace
North Charleston, SC

DEDICATION

This book is dedicated to my parents, my siblings, my children, and all souls who DARE to Believe.

To my father, Pastor Willie Ezel McCoy, Sr. (1933–2007), God's Miracle Man of Faith and Power. A man, who knew no fear, healed the sick, cast out devils, and commanded the dead to live again! You will always be my role model, my placeholder of faith, and the icon from which I received the mantle that rests on me today.

To my mother, Thelma McCoy, you are the joy that lights my world. You help light my way to success. Your every success was my success. If ever any woman dared to believe, Mom, it was you. Your incredible display of faith in God has made believers out of all eleven of your children.

To my siblings, Lue, Willie, LaVern, Ranea, Calvin, Denise, Vanessa, Venice, Enoch, and Letisha, you taught me individuality. You all broke the mold by setting the example to do more and go further. Thank you for trusting the God in me. As you know, the McCoy family has seen firsthand, from the youngest to the oldest, the Miracle-Working Power of God, because our parents dared to believe.

To my children, Kendrick and Kharis, you are the angels that God sent me to help me believe. Thank you for all the times you allowed me to be away from you to help others believe. You both gave me the strength and courage to keep believing everyday. "Mommy, have you finished your book yet?" you'd ask. Because of your enthusiasm, I can say, "I've finished the book!" I am thankful for every hug, kiss, smile, and words of encouragement. Mommy loves you both.

To the Dare to Believe International team, you work hard and give unselfishly. Thank you. Your support, trust, and love helped me DARE to Believe. You helped make "Mission AFRICA 2009" and "Mission ITALY 2011" possible. Thank you for sticking with the vision through hard times. And YES, we will continue to see R.A.W. Miracles (Real Alive Witnesses)!

To all my friends and family who never stopped believing in me, thank you. You are true supporters, and I appreciate your sincere prayers.

CONTENTS

CONTENTS

PART II: INTERNAL DARE

PART III: FAITH

PART IV: PARTNER WITH DESTINY

FOREWORD

top for a moment, look around, and ponder this question. Of all the people you know, what separates the successful ones from those not so successful? It is easy to see that many people are in the big lights, on magazine covers, and making the news—often known as movers and shakers. We can also see and read about those who, for whatever reason, have decided to give up, give in, and give over. Dropout, walk out, quit, divorce, and suicide are common subjects of late. People are exhibiting the signs of doubt, hopelessness, and despair when it comes to considering their options and their future.

Who can we trust, how can we survive, and what will stand the test of time are questions of utmost importance. In today's society we are constantly exposed to the challenges of navigating a distressed worldwide economy, failing education system, dwindling family and moral values, and fast food mentality worship services. In many cases we have perfected the worship service and refined it to a tee. Start on time, end on time, with all the appropriate filling in between to make it warm and inviting for all. What is missing, most times, is the demonstration of the supernatural. The Bible is clear in the book of Mark 16:17–18 *"And these signs shall follow them that believe; In my name shall they cast out devils; they shall speak with new tongues; They shall take up serpents; and if they drink any deadly thing, it shall not hurt them; they shall lay hands on the sick, and they shall recover."* It is not up to the church alone to create an atmosphere for God to work the supernatural; it is the right and privilege of all believers to see their God of creation creating. If we are indeed created in His image, we should be cocreators with the Creator.

Dare to Believe is the challenge put forward to address any of today's problems. No matter what great inventions and modern technology have been engineered, some things, simply put, cannot be improved upon. Faith is the key that unlocks the door to our greater future, and it is essential that we believe. This book lists practical ways to improve on the measure of faith that we already have. Here you will find personal testimony, exercises, and thought-provoking, Bible-based examples that will cause you to recognize your self-imposed limits, which can be removed if only you Dare to Believe.

Because we are sensual beings, to be successful, thrive, and survive, we find ourselves reliant upon what we see, hear, smell, taste, and feel in the physical world. Many self-help books have listed formulas with tangible elements to achieve greatness. What you will find missing in most of these books, however, is the foundation for building success—Belief.

Dare to Believe lays a foundation for which any venture, dream, or project can be built upon. Believing is the one thing that has to remain when one must to go back to the drawing board to start all over again. Believing is the essential ground work that must be laid before the first building blocks are placed. All things are possible to them that believe and even mountains can be moved if we believe.

Belief does not have a prerequisite or disqualifier. Belief does not need a minimum balance, cosigner, good credit, or credit limit to be activated. Belief does not discriminate against gender, race, age, social, economic, or educational status. It works for the rich and the poor, the high and the low, the sick and the well. The novice as well as the veteran believer will immediately benefit from this book. Even Judas, after betraying Jesus, would have benefited from the resurrected savior's salvation had he continued to believe. Judas did no more than many of us, but as long as we have life and breathe there is always an opportunity to rebound and excel if we never allow doubt to be the captain of our destiny ship. I know that you will enjoy, benefit, and grow from the time-tested wisdom written on the pages within this book. I Dare you to take it seriously, take it personally, and take it thoughtfully. I Dare you to Believe!

Rev. Dr. W. G. Hardy, Jr.
Highland Christian Center
United Church of Christ
Portland, Oregon

INTRODUCTION

Journal the Journey

"Write thee all the words that I have spoken unto thee in a book."
JEREMIAH 30:2

"*Jeremiah 30:1...finish the book!*" *was the text message I received from my sister, Dr. Venice L. McCoy, July 16, 2010. I had finished the manuscript March 4, 2010, but needed to edit it, and for some reason I was procrastinating. After she sent me the text, my faith was reignited, and I began to put my hand to the plow and complete what God had given me in February of 2009. The faith journey can be sometimes a challenging one. It is necessary to chronicle this daring walk of faith so that others may gain knowledge, inspiration, and the power to explore the possibilities. Thus, here's my finished product. I pray that it causes you to move with expectation utilizing your faith without limits.*

I remember when I had my first child in January of 1999. I had carried him for eight months, and because of complications during my pregnancy, he was born premature. Despite the challenges, I was so happy that the day had finally come. I couldn't believe he was actually here, breathing, moving in my arms and mine after 33 hours of hard labor! Beholding his nearly bald head, gray eyes, gorgeous smile, and bright skin with tiny feet and fingers made it all worth it. But then I was filled with so much anxiety and the unknown about how to nurture and care for him. It was almost overwhelming. I had to tell myself, "Evelyn, you can do this." I had to believe no matter what challenges came my way; with the help of God, all things were possible.

From the cradle to adolescence, we teach our children to believe. When they first learn how to walk, we encourage them and say, "come on, you can do it," stretching our hands toward them in confidence that they will walk. Although they fall many times before they perfect walking, we still encourage them through every fall. Similarly, God the Father helps guide our course, daring us through every difficult situation to BELIEVE. Whether major or minor, our past challenging experiences *and* accomplishments constantly serve as a reminder to believe again and again.

This book is intended to help awaken, utilize, and/or increase your faith in areas you may have never thought possible. You will find during the course of your reading biblical examples of the patriarchs of faith, scriptural supporting references regarding faith, and accounts of my own walk of faith. We will explore dare from an external and internal perspective and how it relates to your faith, define various dimensions of faith and what relevance it has in your life, and discover how partnering with destiny enhances the materialization of your dreams. This book is in no way a total compilation of all there is to know about faith but a glimpse of how you can use your God-given faith to make monumental strides in every area of your life.

Upon your completion of this faith guide, it is my hope that you will have unlocked and unleashed a whole new world of possibilities regarding your destiny and belief in God. You will discover embodied throughout your reading several themes classified in the following areas that are linked to your faith: emotional healing, physical health, economic growth, social change, psychological cure, interpersonal strength, spiritual definition, and organizational development. Because God has created you as a multidimensional being, all of these facets of your life are relevant to your destiny and directly linked to your faith. They are a part of you; every part makes the whole cohesive. Get ready to transcend all barriers or prohibitions that may have served as an impediment to you in the past. With an open heart and mind, see yourself in the pages utilizing your faith to realize your dreams.

A Faith Intercept

Dare to go beyond what's "normal." Believe God for the invisible. *"And the earth was without form, and void; and darkness was upon the face of the deep," Genesis 1:2.* When God spoke in faith, He intercepted emptiness, in the invisible realm, knowing that something was going to materialize in the natural. *"All things were made by him; and without him was not any thing made that was made," John 1:3.* God did not want the earth to stay as it was—empty, dark, and lifeless. So God spoke: commanding light, creating life, and exemplifying love. You to can speak a faith intercept into the invisible realms and see the manifestation of your faith come into fruition, bringing about drastic positive change in your life and the lives of others, exploring a level of love unknown to many.

Faith will cause you to display unselfish love encouraging others to come out of their comfort zones. Many people remain in their comfort zones because they are not required to reach or stretch to enlarge their place of habitation. Don't allow the normalcy of fear and unbelief hold you hostage. Sometimes **God will push you to your place of growth by causing you to experience *external* turbulence.** Situations outside of your control may have happened or is happening to you. Don't take this as a sign that God doesn't love you, but realize reaching requires movement and stretching sometimes hurts. God has designed you to accomplish all things through Christ who strengthens you, so don't give up just because things get a little shaky. *"God hath dealt to every man the measure of faith,"* Romans 12:3. **HE created every creature with an *internal* ability to reach, with assured power, beyond what natural limits define.**

Peter, a disciple of Jesus, was a great example of this. *"And in the fourth watch of the night Jesus went unto them, walking on the sea. And when the disciples saw him walking on the sea, they were troubled, saying, It is a spirit; and they cried out for fear. But straightway Jesus spake unto them, saying, Be of good cheer; it is I; be not afraid. And Peter answered him and said, Lord, if it be thou, bid me to come unto thee on the water. And he said, Come. And when Peter was come down out of the ship, he walked on the water, to go to Jesus,"* Matthew 14:25–29.

Peter acted in faith, daring to believe that it was Jesus as He so identified and that he too could walk on water. The challenge was on both sides of the ship: Internally, Peter asked Jesus if it's really him (a demand for identification) "bid me to come." Externally, Jesus challenged Peter in His response by saying, "Come." He believed it was Jesus, going beyond what natural limits defined.

Several natural limitations *could have* stopped Peter from believing: (1) By the laws of physics, humans don't walk on water. (2) It was dark (the fourth watch, three to six a.m.)—who wants to try new things in darkness? (3) The winds were contrary and waves tossed. He could have said, "No way, absolutely not!" Peter dared to believe in Jesus, himself, and his future, leaving the others in the ship. **You must come to a point in your life where you step into the unknown to discover your untapped potential, which is not predicated upon someone else's belief.**

It wasn't until Peter began to look at the elements around him that he began to sink. *"But when he saw the wind boisterous, he was afraid; and beginning to sink, he cried, saying Lord, save me," verse 30.* Peter stepped out of the ship and realized this isn't the "norm" (to walk on water), and fear overtook him. *"And immediately Jesus stretched forth his hand, and caught him, and said unto him, O thou of little faith, wherefore didst thou doubt? And when they were come into the ship, the wind ceased. Then they that were in the ship came and worshipped him, saying, Of a truth thou are the Son of God," verses 31–33.* Note that Peter's act of faith caused the other disciples to *believe* that Jesus was the Son of God. What acts of faith are causing others to believe in your circle of friends, neighborhood, city, and region or globally?

(The following references show several reasons why, when walking on the water, Peter should have not doubted Jesus's ability to perform miracles and command the impossible. As you review each incident, consider the questions that follow and its relevance to how God may be challenging you to do greater things.)

We will also look at how Peter's daring excursion on the Sea of Galilee helped shape his faith in God to do the miraculous after Jesus's ascension into heaven:

- Jesus had an unblemished track record of performing miracles: why was walking on water any different? He had just performed the miraculous feeding of five thousand souls with only five loaves of bread and two fishes. He had calmed the Sea of Galilee in Matthew 8 when the disciples were on board the ship with Him. What miracles in your past has God performed for you?

- Peter had personally witnessed the miraculous works of the Son of God. Jesus healed Peter's mother-in-law when she was sick of a fever (Matt. 8:14–15). He also healed the woman who was diseased with an issue of blood for twelve years (Matt. 9:20–22). He raised a certain ruler's daughter from the dead in the same chapter, in addition to performing many other miracles. Now, recall and analyze how God brought you through your past personal challenges to realize that your present situation is no different.

- Peter became afraid and was "beginning to sink." This did indicate unbelief and/or doubt, but this also was an indication that at some point and time, there was faith. When responding in faith to the call of Jesus, you will step into the unknown. Once you experience the unfamiliar, you may encounter external disturbances. You may even perceive the opposition as a discouragement, but it is recommended that

you do as Peter did—call on Jesus for your help. Ask yourself, has the unknown caused me to sink or use my faith?

🌀 Once Jesus stretched out His hand and caught him, Peter
still had to use his faith to walk on water back to the ship.
From that moment forward, Peter had something the rest of
the disciples hadn't experienced, unsinkable faith. You may
say, "But he did sink." In a sense, yes, but he did not drown.
He had the faith that Jesus could save him and cried out,
"Lord, save me." You have to know your faith will rescue
you from a seemingly sinking impossibility. Ponder these
questions: Do I possess unsinkable faith during my stormy
situations? Do I allow my faith to continue to operate during turbulent times, or does fear overtake me?

🌀 Peter's faith defied the laws of matter and the impossible.
And matter (water) didn't matter when his faith was in operation. After Jesus's ascension to heaven, Peter received the
power of the Holy Ghost in Acts the first chapter *("But ye
shall receive power after that the Holy Ghost is come upon you..."
Acts 1:8)* after which, he performed many miracles. He
healed the lame man at the gate called Beautiful in Acts 3,
a notable miracle visible to all who dwelt in Jerusalem and
could not be denied. Many sick people were brought into
the streets of Jerusalem on beds and couches, according to
Acts 5:15 that they might be healed by the passing of Peter's
shadow. Now that's powerful. Have you received the power
of the Holy Ghost causing you to perform the miraculous
through faith?

⑨ He went further with his assured belief of faith in Jesus Christ and raised Tabitha of Joppa from the dead in Acts 9. God acknowledged the faith of Peter and answered his prayers. Dare to believe all things are possible and use your God-given faith without limits. Are there dead situations in your life that need to be raised? Have you aligned your faith with the word of God to see the manifestation of miracles? Will your faith triumph?

This miracle of walking on water was the turning point of Peter's faith in God. What is yours? Peter's walk of daring faith on the Sea of Galilee, and post-Galilee, reveal in its interwoven fabric unlocked and unleashed, the aforementioned themes reflecting his belief in God. With every attempt to **DARE to Believe**, you will have external and internal influences that will try to stop you (more to come on internal and external challenges). But I encourage you to keep Matthew 19:26 in your heart, *"with God all things are possible."*

Cross-Country Challenge

My most vivid external experience of daring to believe beyond what natural limits defined was to trust God's purpose and plan for my life when He told me to move from Illinois to Oregon in November of 2006. I told God yes I'll move, with certain prerequisites. Yes, I was out of my mind telling God I'll obey IF! If you provide me with a good-paying job, a house not an apartment, good neighborhood, and great church home, I'll move. God was challenging my faith, daring me to move beyond the level of faith I was used to operating in. In

August of 2007, I took the leap of faith and journeyed toward the West Coast into the land of the unfamiliar.

While on the road with two small children, the promising job and home fell through. I had had four interviews with this company and was positive this was a sure thing. The company said their financial portfolio prohibited them from hiring me at that time. I was six hours away from Oregon with no job and no place to live. Just before getting the call about the job and housing, I remember talking to my Dad, and he asked, "Is everything ok?" I responded, "Everything is fine."

After getting the disappointing call from the company, I looked out the window of my car toward heaven despite the external challenges, believed internally that it was all orchestrated by the Father, and said "God, I still trust you." Here I was transitioning cross-country with no tangible resources in sight. Then I realized that I had one critical resource, and that was *faith in God to dare to believe* that He would make what was an apparent disaster into orchestrated destiny.

I had to align my will with the will and plan of the Father and dare to believe Him for the impossible. With each step of faith God continued to show Himself strong in my life. I had to believe God on a whole different level. He pushed me out of my comfort zone (living in Chicago with the support of family and friends) to a strange place (Portland, where He could stretch my faith). God was calling me out of the *familiar place of believing* to a realm of belief. God will test our faith to see if we truly trust Him regardless of things being chaotic in our lives. He paid no attention to my prerequisites; He was looking at my heart (place of decision making) to see if I would "step out of the ship."

God has shown me so much since that time. I believe in Him against all odds. I believe that I am capable through Him of attaining my goals in life (including writing this book). I believe in my future striving every day to reach beyond the now. I believe that someone will be inspired to change their course of destiny after reading this book. I believe.

Your destiny doesn't stop at problems or even attained goals but keeps on developing as your faith grows and opens the door to and for so many others. This book is designed for the preschooler to those that hold a PhD. The preschooler will not understand the language, but those who read the book will pass the information to them in another usable form. Your ability to believe affects more than just yourself; it affects those who are watching you.

My son and daughter have been watching me since their birth, and as they grow from adolescence into adulthood, they will continue to see if I am utilizing the same faith I taught them from the cradle. Likewise, the disciples were watching to see what Peter would do, and as a result of his going beyond natural limits, they believed that Jesus was the Son of God.

This book will do the following:

- ☉ Challenge you to believe in God in the face of minor and major opposition whether it is natural or spiritual;
- ☉ DARE you to be valiant, facing external challenges and releasing internal courage with resilient faith;
- ☉ Give you impacting transferable tools on how to use your God-given faith without limits in every area of your life;
- ☉ Encourage and motivate you to believe in yourself and partner with destiny;

🌀 Provoke you to unlock and unleash your faith and embrace the fulfillment of your dreams *every day.*

Come go with me on a *Dare to Believe* journey!

PART I

External Dare

∿

"Only be thou strong and very courageous…that thou mayest prosper wither-sover thou goest. …thou shalt have good success."
JOSHUA 1:7–8

God spoke these words to Joshua, the son of Nun, Moses's minister, field commander, personal aid, and successor when He charged him to possess the land of Canaan—flowing with milk and honey. Canaan was Israel's in accordance with God's promise in both the Abrahamic and Mosaic covenants. God said to Joshua, *"Now therefore arise, go over this Jordan, thou, and all this people, unto the land which I do give to them, even to the children of Israel," Joshua 1:2.* God had orchestrated this direct external dare given to Joshua. Accepting this challenge would give him and the children of Israel direct access to prosperity and success.

External means coming from the outside. God was the external vehicle through which Joshua would take possession of the Promised

Land. God had already deeded Canaan to him and the children of Israel. There are a multiplicity of deeds coming from an outside source (God) that has been promised to you and your offspring. It is up to you to operate in courage and gain possession of them.

Dare means to challenge to perform an action especially as a proof of courage. The two key words are action and courage. Alan Cohen penned, "It takes a lot of courage to release the familiar and seemingly secure, to embrace the new. But there is no real security in what is no longer meaningful. There is more security in the adventurous and exciting, for in movement there is life, and in change there is power."

God (external) was challenging (dare) Joshua to perform an action. Joshua and the children of Israel were about to embark upon new territory that God had promised was already theirs. It was the right time for Joshua to be appointed to this assignment because Moses was dead. The power of change had taken effect. Joshua was not only given this assignment as a proof of courage but as a true sign that he believed God. God, in His chosen timing, is trying to get new blessings to you, but you must release the familiar, be willing to stretch (move) your faith (power), and possess the courage needed for the challenge. Begin to confess that you have the power to perform the challenge. You can say something like, "God, I thank you that you have given me the ability to take on this challenge. I dare to believe you for the impossible. I believe your word, and your word says I cannot fail because you are with me."

Reach outside of your sphere seeing the possibilities awaiting you. Adopt the spirit of faith, believing in a hope greater than you.

In this section, we will analyze three forms of external challenges:

1. Orchestrated by God. There are times when God challenges you to move beyond the realm of belief in Him that you've been accustomed to operating in.

2. Solicited by Satan. Satan will challenge your faith in God by causing what seems to be external turbulence characterized by chaotic stochastic changes. It is then that you must diffuse His momentum through utilization of your faith in the Almighty stabilizing the course of courage. Satan wants to deplane your faith in God, and He also wants to hydroplane your faith causing you to lose directional control. Do not allow the turbulence to scare you into fainting or succumbing to His tactics.

3. Initiated by human will. Sometimes people will challenge you not to believe in God, yourself, and your destiny. Hit the mute button and keep on watching God take you from faith to faith and from glory to glory even as a result of their direct challenge of your belief.

All three are designed to stretch and shape your faith leading you down the path of attained spiritual and natural success. We will look at biblical examples of both giving credence as to why an external dare is necessary for spiritual growth and natural stabilization.

To help maintain control and direction, you will be given some tactical methods, tools, strategies, antidotes, and promises through the word of God to help direct and stretch your faith during turbulent times. You will need these instruments of faith throughout the course of your journey called life. Create a challenge journal so that you may look back in retrospect taking account of obtained successes and learning curves.

Challenges will come, but they are for your making. Whether orchestrated by God, solicited by Satan, or initiated by human will, these challenges are meant to strengthen your faith and perfect God's will and plan for your life. The external dare is designed to provoke you into enlarging the place of your tent, lengthening your cords, and strengthening your stakes, Isaiah 54:2.

CHAPTER ONE

Challenges Orchestrated by God

God's plan for Joshua required him to enlarge, lengthen, strengthen, and stretch his faith beyond any realm he'd ever experienced before—to bring His chosen people into the land of promise. Likewise, God has promised you rewards for your obedience of faith—land for which you did not labor, cities that you did not build, and vineyards that you did not plant, Joshua 24:13. Embrace courage and go possess the promise in faith with the authority God has given you. The dimensions of your faith are measured by your obedience to God. God's intention for challenging Joshua was one of promise and fulfillment. Without fail God will continue to show you just how faithful He is when you step into the unknown daring to believe.

The dimensions of your faith are measured by your obedience to God.

Joshua went into unknown territory by faith. God had given him clear instructions, *"turn not from it to the right hand or to the left,"* *Joshua 1:7,* and he obeyed God's command to the letter. Because of his spiritual obedience, he conquered many battles as he seized the land of promise including Jericho. Jericho was a strategic Canaanite stronghold, the oldest known city in ancient Canaan, and its age and location made it a prominent city in that region. He sent spies into the land of Jericho, possessed it, and crossed Jordan on dry land.

Along the way to your destiny, you may have to cross some "Jordan rivers" and conquer "Jerichos." Utilize your faith as did Joshua and the priests that carried the Ark of the Covenant. They obeyed God, and as soon as the feet of the priests were dipped into the brim of the river Jordan, the waters split and stood straight up on both sides, and all the Israelites walked across on dry land. No obstacle is too deep or too high for God Almighty!

Although an external dare brings with it opposition, conflict, and spiritual warfare, it brings rewards as well—it builds character, marks faith as a defense, and releases supernatural ability. Joshua encountered formidable situations but counteracted them through faith by displaying the courage God had told him to embrace. When you encounter external challenges, release the zeal of faith with authority knowing that your God is with you.

Joshua was faithful to God's plan and will concerning his destiny and that of the children of Israel. His faithfulness to Moses's direction, as his predecessor, is constantly underscored as well. This external dare provoked him to unlock and unleash the foundation of faith that was ingrained in him by Moses. *"Faith cometh by hearing, and hearing by the word of God,"* *Romans 10:17.* He heard the word of faith spoken by Moses and was one of the twelve spies that Moses sent into Canaan to spy out the land in Numbers 13. Joshua and Caleb came back with a good report saying they were well able to take the land while the others murmured, "We are as grasshoppers in our sight and theirs." When you reverence God as your ultimate leader and acknowledge His choice vessel as such, your reward is guaranteed and the benefits are unprecedented.

Joshua experienced natural stabilization, the *benefits* of daring to believe. <u>Interpersonal and social change</u>, *"So the Lord was with Joshua; and his fame was noised throughout all the country," Joshua 6:27.* <u>Psychological cure</u>, after the fall of Jericho, Joshua no longer struggled in his mind about forthcoming victories. <u>Economic growth</u>, *"And the Lord gave unto Israel all the land which he sware to give unto their fathers; and they possessed it, and dwelt therein," Joshua 21:43.* <u>Emotional healing</u>, *"And the Lord said unto Joshua, This day have I rolled away the reproach (shameful captivity) of Egypt from off you," Joshua 5:9.* <u>Physical health</u>, Joshua lived a full life reaching 110 years old. <u>Spiritual definition</u>, *"As for me and my house, we will serve the Lord," Joshua 24:15.* Imagine what benefits await you as you embrace an external dare orchestrated by God.

Joshua repeatedly triumphed over all his enemies leading the children of Israel into the Promise Land. He possessed all the land including Gibeon. He along with the children of Israel operated in faith causing God to act mightily on their behalf. This was a pivotal point in Joshua's belief in God commanding the sun and moon to be still until they avenged themselves upon their enemies. God hearkened unto the voice of Joshua because he operated in faith and with courage. You may have to fight several battles when God challenges you to dare to believe.

Know this, God is with you through every battleground experience cheering you on, and with certainty you will win the war. *"So Joshua took all that land, the hills, and all the south country, and all the land of Goshen, and the valley, and the plain, and the mountain of Israel, and the valley of the same," Joshua 11:16.* God has promised you prosperity and good success; it belongs to you.

Know this, God is with you through every battleground experience cheering you on, and with certainty you will win the war.

Today, God is saying to you DARE to Believe! God's promises to you cannot manifest until you take action. Joshua's faith caused them to take action. Faith becomes active when you do. That may sound simple but it's true. Until I actually moved in faith from my comfort zone of "familiar faith" to a place of stretching into the unknown "daring faith," my faith was dormant. *"Faith without works is dead," according to James 2:20.* I had to leave Chicago and find out what God was saying regarding my future, my destiny. I had to move my faith in the direction that God was pointing, not just physically but spiritually. You too may have to leave some place, things, or people to take your faith to the next dimension.

Take Abraham for example. He experienced an external dare when the Lord spoke to him, *"Get thee out of thy country, and from thy kindred, and from thy father's house, unto a land that I will show thee: And I will make of thee a great nation, and I will bless thee and make thy name great; and thou shalt be a blessing," Genesis 12:1–2.* Look at all the rewards and benefits God promises Abram for his obedience. Abram (before

God changed his name to Abraham) is a great illustration of how God challenges you to move from the place of the familiar and trust Him regardless of how comfortable you are there. When Lot (his nephew) departed from Abram, the Lord then said to him, *"Lift up now thine eyes, and look from the place where thou art northward, and southward, and eastward, and westward: For all the land which thou seest, to thee will I give it, and to thy seed for ever," Genesis 13:14–15.*

God gave Abram some clear instructions. God told Abram to look up, move from where he was, and in every direction the land was his and his descendants. You must consciously choose to obey God to the letter because it will cause greatness to be yours continually. Abraham was not only presented with the challenge to obey God and move from his father's house but also offering up Isaac his son. *"And Abraham stretched forth his hand, and took the knife to slay his son. And the angel of the Lord called unto him out of heaven, and said, Abraham, Abraham: and he said, Here am I. And he said, Lay not thine hand upon the lad, neither do thou any thing unto him: for now I know that thou fearest God, seeing thou hast not withheld thy son, thine only son from me," Genesis 22:10–12.* God may be requiring you to sacrifice some things testing your faith in Him. Don't be afraid.

When you take on a dare, you're taking a stance of belief. You're saying, "I can do this! I may have some challenging moments, but they won't last a lifetime." **Life threw me some curve balls, but I learned how to catch the balls in the curve and redirect the direction, motion, and momentum of my destiny with God's help.**

CHAPTER TWO

Challenges Solicited by Satan

We have looked at the rewards, benefits, and triumph of an external dare orchestrated by God to help bring you to a place of prosperity, success, and complete trust in Him. Now let's examine external challenges through the solicitation of Satan. We will explore how these solicitations will ultimately catapult your faith in God to the next realm. Job was a star example.

God said to Satan, *"Hast thou considered my servant Job, that there is none like him in the earth, a perfect and an upright man, one that feareth God, and escheweth evil?" Job 1:8.* God had complete confidence that Job would remain faithful to Him even while being tested. God is challenging you to be faithful to Him through your tests and the trials as was Job.

Note Satan had already inquired of Job beforehand because he told God, *"Hast not thou made a hedge about him, and about his house, and about all that he hath on every side? Thou hast blessed the work of his hands, and his substance is increased in the land," Job 1:10.* In the same way, Satan has inquired about you. He's checked your faith needle to see if it points in the "strong faith" direction or the "weak faith" zone. He's monitored your reactions to success and disappointment.

Satan solicited God to challenge Job. He said to God take away all that he has and he'll curse you to your face. God responded, *"All that he hath is in thy power," Job 1:12.* Satan had to get permission from God to challenge Job, and he did so twice. Satan is not self-created; therefore, He must get permission from His Creator in order to do anything.

Satan is seeking opportunities to petition God concerning you and your destiny. Do not be alarmed if God allows Satan to challenge you. God has well equipped you to win every battleground experience and ultimately the war. God has given you the faith to overcome every obstacle. *"Nay in all these things we are more than conquerors through him that loved us," Romans 8:37.* All these things, meaning challenges (tribulation, distress, peril, or persecution). These external challenges are used as vehicles of faith ensuring that you truly trust God throughout life's journey. The scriptures tell us not to put our trust in uncertain riches but in the living God neither lean to the arms of flesh. Job had great wealth and was challenged by Satan to see if he would curse God if he lost it all.

During Job's time of being challenged by Satan, He caused his sheep to be burned up, servants to be slain, and children to be destroyed by a great wind causing their house to fall upon them. Before Job could finish receiving one report of bad news from the servant that escaped Satan's hand, another would come with more bad news. It may seem that you are being bombarded with personal challenges one after another. Don't let fear grip you. Reach beyond what is tangible and tap into the intangible realm of faith. Your faith will then materialize causing your circumstances to change in your favor.

Don't let fear grip you.

Ironically, it was Job's wife who suggested that he do what Satan had predicted, *"Dost thou still retain thine integrity? curse God and die,"* *Job 2:9.* This she told him after Satan had come the second time and struck his body, covering it with sore boils. It may be that the closest person to you is suggesting that you abort the promises of God through unbelief and blasphemy. Don't bow. **Despite the extremely difficult challenges and the greatness of his grief, Job sinned not with his lips nor charged God foolishly.**

Satan brought evil upon Job and thought he would cause him to curse God, lose his faith in God, and be separated from God. The challenge worked in reverse causing Job to say, *"All the days of my appointed time will I wait, till my change come,"* *Job 14:14.* After seven days of silence and mourning with Job, his so-called friends even challenged his faith in God, accusing him of sin. Job goes on to say, *"Though he slay me, yet will I trust in him,"* *Job 13:15.*

When challenges come, continue to trust God no matter what the odds look like. "Friends" may think they are doing or saying the right thing in their eyes but know that the eyes of the Lord looks over the righteous and His ear is inclined unto you. Job stated his faith in God to his friends, *"For I know that my Redeemer liveth, and that he shall stand at the latter day upon the earth,"* *Job 19:25.* From the depths of degradation, Job referred to God as one who will champion his cause and vindicate him. Job suffered at the hands of Satan and the heart-staking words of his wife and friends. But he maintained his integrity and faith in God and uttered, *"All the while my breath is in me, and the spirit of God is in my nostrils; My lips shall not speak wickedness, nor my tongue utter deceit," Job 27:3–4.*

Job's humanistic character caused him to inquire of God through prayer *why* this great tumult had befallen him. At some point in your life, you may ask the question "why me" or "what have I done to deserve this?" God finally responded to Job out of a whirlwind in the form of eighty-three questions in which Job could not answer one of them.

God questioned Job about the existence of the world, cosmos, animals, and human life. God asked Job who waters the earth where no man dwells? God said, *"Shall he that contendeth with the Almighty instruct him? He that reproveth God, let him answer it," Job 40:2.* In other words God was saying He is alpha and omega, and His wisdom is far above that of any man. Again, God will allow turbulence to come into your life so that you will realize that you need Him. Job submitted to God's will and plan for his life.

God will cause those who persecute you to come and ask for forgiveness and not only that but help enrich you. The Lord told Job's friends that they had not spoken things that were right as did Job. He told them to ask Job for forgiveness and bring him an offering and that he was going to pray for them. *"And the Lord turned the captivity of Job, when he prayed for his friends: also the Lord gave Job twice as much as he had before," Job 42:10.* It may be one of the hardest things to do when your friends have spoken evil against you, but pray for them and watch God restore you better than you were in your first state.

"So the Lord blessed the latter end of Job more than his beginning," Job 42:12. When God allows you to face challenges, know that its

purpose is shaping the holistic man or woman—physically, spiritually, mentally, and financially. We can conclude and glean the following from Job's experience:

1. Your righteousness does not exclude you from external Satanic challenges. Job was a perfect and an upright man.

2. During your challenge, remain faithful to God who is able to bring you out of them. Job did not curse God with his lips.

3. Don't allow people to extract from your faith and begin to question God about His capabilities. It was Job's friends that planted questions in Job's mind about "why God?"

4. Pray for your enemies. It was only after Job prayed for his friends that God turned his captivity.

5. God will give you double what you had in the beginning.

6. Job lived to see the fourth generation of his seed being full of days.

When God allows you to face challenges know that its purpose is shaping the holistic man or woman— physically, spiritually, mentally, and financially.

When you are facing external challenges, examine whether it is God orchestrated or a Satanic solicitation. This will help you in your approach to the challenges, and your approach is important. How you handle your challenge is directly linked to your success. You must have faith in God, obedience rather than sacrifice, courage to conquer, pray without ceasing, and the ability to fast. These attributes will enforce the purpose and plan of God concerning your challenge.

First ask the question, what is the purpose of this challenge? Second, what am I suppose to learn and/or gain from it? Third, what are the rewards and/or benefits? Challenges are meant to grow your faith causing you to reach relentless (i.e., Joshua) and unquenchable (i.e., Job) faith. See yourself triumphant. God doesn't orchestrate or allow you to go through challenges for nothing. Whether God orchestrated or allowed, you are guaranteed victory and an insurmountable amount of natural and supernatural increase. Whatever challenges you are facing it is not meant to take you out but empower you to dare to believe God.

You might ask what if the challenge is neither orchestrated nor allowed by God but an outright attack of the enemy plotting against you. You must know how to embrace God's plan and circumvent the enemy's plot. Ask yourself: is this external challenge in alignment with the word of God? If the answer is no, then it must be a plot from Satan and for your demise. Then you must fortify yourself knowing that you have weapons of faith employed and sharpened especially and specifically designed for the enemy. The enemy may challenge you to give up on your hopes and dreams. Don't buy into it. Only believe.

The remainder of this section will: look at some in-depth biblical examples of external challenges expressed in the form of human will. Then, specific tools needed for the challenge, next, being strategically positioned for the challenge, and the ultimate challenge—believing the promises of God. Sometimes people will try to hinder the plan of God for your life. You must at all costs anchor your faith in God knowing that storms may come but in the end you are the champion of victory. Open your heart, mind, and spirit to receive some vital information needed for your faith journey.

CHAPTER THREE

Challenges Initiated by Human Will

Quick review, *external dare* is a challenge coming from an outside source to perform an action, especially as a proof of coverage. This type of dare tests your faith in God and yourself, unveils any areas of weakness and doubt, and releases a powerfully strong anointing that others will see and begin to believe in their own vision, destiny, and purpose. It causes you to develop a more intimate relationship with your Creator through battleground experiences. Following is an external challenge that presents itself (via Goliath, i.e., Human will) and gives God the opportunity to show His chosen people once again that faith in action will always conquer fear. As you face external challenges via human will (those who take it upon themselves to challenge you), consider the tactical methods and tools that the shepherd boy used during his dare.

David, the son of Jesse, accepted this type of dare in the first book of Samuel the seventeenth chapter. The Philistines were in battle

with the men of Israel. David was daring and took on the challenge
of the champion Goliath out of the camp of the Philistines. Goliath
was well over nine feet tall, and his armor and weaponry weighed over
150 pounds. Verses 4–7 describes his dress code as having a helmet
of brass, a coat of mail, greaves of brass upon his legs, and the staff
of his spear was like a weaver's beam; and his spear's head weighed
six hundred shekels of iron. Goliath was the experienced picture of
a champion. On the contrary, David—a youth, ruddy and of a fair
countenance—did not appear to have the qualifications of a soldier.
But what he did have was courage, confidence, and faith born out of
the experience of God's previous deliverances on his behalf.

*"And the Philistine said, I defy (challenge, dare) the armies of Israel this
day; give me a man, that we may fight together,"* I Samuel 17:10. Goliath
gives a direct challenge to anyone who would accept it, unknowing
that he would meet his ultimate challenger (who was a boy not a
man). *"And all the men of Israel, when they saw the man, fled from him,
and were sore afraid," verse 24.* But David dared to be different and believed. *"And David spake to the men that stood by him, saying, What shall
be done to the man that killeth this Philistine, and taketh away the reproach
from Israel? for who is this uncircumcised Philistine, that he should defy the
armies of the living God?" verse 26.* David was so confident in his God
that he was going to defeat Goliath that he wanted to know what the
reward was. The reward was threefold: *"The king would enrich him with
great riches, and will give him his daughter and make his father's house free
in Israel," verse 25.*

All that stood by heard the words of David. Verse 28 says that
David's eldest brother Eliab's anger was kindled against him and he
said, "Why did you come here? With whom have you left those few

sheep you were tending to? I know your pride and insolence of your heart has brought you here to see the battle." People will discourage you repeatedly throughout life to abandon something they think is out of your reach. But when you know God has ordained this external challenge to stretch your faith and give you abundance, face the giant head-on with the spirit of victory. David continued with his proclamation of victory until others told Saul, the king, about it and he sent for him. He petitioned Saul to allow him to go and fight. David proclaimed, *"Thy servant slew both the lion and the bear: and this uncircumcised Philistine shall be as one of them, seeing he hath defied the armies of the living God," verse 36.*

I declare if you stretch: reach beyond natural limits without breaking, God will be the constant link that helps you to reach goal after goal, believing again and again. God wants you to understand that Goliath is only a nine-foot bluff. You have the power to call the enemy's bluff.

Stretch—to reach beyond natural limits without breaking.

By this time, David had made several statements:

1. I am not afraid of the challenge or the people who stand against me.
2. My past successes have given me promise that God will give me victory again.
3. The odds are in my favor because I believe in God against all odds.

There may be a Goliath in your path to success, but I declare giants do fall! Without fail, the enemy will repeatedly bring challenges to you that seem impossible to conquer, but you must continue to be strong and courageous knowing that good success is yours. The Philistine came and presented himself forty days, but the day came when it was his last time. Your perseverance, ability to withstand difficulty, and belief in God through past victories will keep you anchored.

CHAPTER FOUR

Vital Tools Needed for the Challenge

David's preparedness for the battle with Goliath included choosing the right tools. You cannot defeat the Goliaths in your life without the instruments designed to do so. Your victory will manifest through correct use of vital tools. Saul thought David needed his armor to fight Goliath. *"And Saul armed David with his armor, and put a helmet of brass upon his head; also he armed him with a coat of mail,"* verse 38. But David said to Saul, *"I cannot go with these; for I have not proved them. And David put them off him,"* verse 39. David was saying thank you for trying to help, but I'm not sure your weaponry will help me win—these don't fit me. What worked for you may not work for me, and I can't take that risk. There may be those around you who want to help you win, but it may not be a fit for your battle.

Your victory will manifest through correct use of vital tools.

Seek God concerning what tools you need to win the challenge. This is important when you are facing Goliath (giants, obstacles) on your path to success. David was on his way and in preparation to become king. This was his first public challenge (as he would face many before and during his reign), and he needed to know from God exactly what tools to implement, as he was in the lineage that would bring forth the Christ child Jesus. It's important to note that your challenges and successes are not just about you but generations that will come after you. You are daring to believe for people you will never meet.

Verse 40 and 49–51 brings into action the dare in which the Philistine invited and the belief in which David stood: *"And he took his staff in his hand, and chose him five smooth stones out of the brook, and put them in a shepherd's bag which he had, even in a scrip; and his sling was in his hand: and he drew near to the Philistine. And David put his hand in his bag, and took thence a stone, and slang it, and smote the Philistine in his forehead; that the stone sunk into his forehead; and he fell upon his face to the earth. So David prevailed over the Philistine with a sling and with a stone, and smote the Philistine, and slew him, but there was no sword in the hand of David. Therefore David ran, and stood upon the Philistine, and took his sword, and drew it out of the sheath thereof, and slew him, and cut off his head therewith. And when the Philistines saw their champion was dead they fled."*

Let's dissect what happened. David chose five smooth stones. God led him to pick which tools he needed to conquer Goliath because the scripture said he "chose" them. David didn't just pick any stones that were in sight; he was careful to examine what was the perfect fit to defeat his enemy. **Seek God regarding what resources you need** to see the manifestation of your victory; this is important. David only needed one of the five stones taken from the brook to defeat Goliath. God will provide you with more resources than you need to be victorious. Your only assignment is to choose the necessary tools that are God driven.

Seek God regarding what resources you need to see the manifestation of your victory; this is important.

Next point, David withdrew the stone out of a shepherd's bag and had a sling in his hand. The stone and the sling were used as vital tools to defeat the enemy. The stone without the sling would have done him no good, and the sling without the stone would have profited him nothing either. The scripture declares, *"So David prevailed over the Philistine with a sling and with a stone, and smote the Philistine."* It is crucial to **follow the exact instructions of God** when you are on an assignment to believe.

Yes, he who conquered the giant was the keeper of the sheep and the youngest of his father Jesse's eight sons. It does not matter what background you come from, when **God has chosen you** no one else can exclude or eliminate you. The Lord told Samuel, the prophet, not to look on the countenance or stature of whom He'd chosen. *"For man looketh on the outward appearance, but the Lord looketh on the heart,"* I Samuel 16:7. *"Then Samuel took the horn of oil, and anointed him in the midst of his brethren: and the Spirit of the Lord came upon David from that day forward,"* verse 13. David was handpicked by God and anointed for the assignment that was ahead of him right in front of his brothers, who thought he could not meet the challenge. Don't worry about those who are looking to see you fail; keep your focus on the assignment and not the assassin. Remember, God has chosen you, not your enemy.

Don't give the enemy any time to recover from his wound. David ran and stood upon his enemy and used his own sword and cut off his head. Once you recognize the enemy of fear, procrastination, insecurity, or other barriers that keep you from daring to believe are down for the count, cut off its head at the source of its chief origin. Put an end to every distraction that would or could possibly cause you to doubt the possibilities.

Lastly, **the naysayers** who are standing and waiting to see you fail **will scatter.** When the Philistines saw that Goliath was dead, they fled. *"Submit yourselves therefore to God. Resist the devil and he will flee from you," James 4:7.* David was submitted wholly to the Father; his resistance came in the form of God-given tools, and the enemy fled.

See your victory on the other side of the giant as did David. His faith was in action! He became a national hero and the greatest king of Israel because he believed without limits. He did not allow Goliath's stature and past victories intimidate him. You must see your victory on the other side of the challenge and use the vital tools God has given you to conquer your enemy (fear, procrastination, and unbelief).

In brief,

- Seek God regarding what resources you need;
- Follow the exact instructions of God;
- Remember, God has chosen you;
- Don't give the enemy any time to recover;
- The naysayers will scatter;
- See your victory.

CHAPTER FIVE

Strategically Positioned for the Challenge

Let's study one more example of an external dare and go deeper. Remember dare means to challenge to perform an action, especially as a proof of courage. We've discussed that God will cause external turbulence to push you to the next realm of belief, allow the enemy to challenge you, and people as well. The Goliaths in your faith walk do fall when using the necessary tools; now you must be positioned for the challenge.

God will allow the enemy to help push you to the next dimension of your being, the next realm of your existence, the place where He wants you to be. You are probably saying, "Wait a minute. My enemy is going to help land me right in the middle of God's plan for me?" Yes. Take Jesus for example. If the enemy knew that Jesus would die for our sins and free us from sin, He would have never solicited His crucifixion through the chief priests, high priests, scribes, elders, and the Sanhedrin. Jesus was strategically positioned for the challenge unbeknown to the enemy.

"For David himself said by the Holy Ghost, The Lord said to my Lord, sit thou on my right hand, till I make thine enemies thy footstool," Mark 12:36. In other words, God said to David, "Sit down right here by me and rest (position yourself) until I make everyone who wouldn't support you, support you, everyone who said you wouldn't make it reverse their declaration and become your publicist."

Every time you dare to believe, God sees your faith and says, "Rest while I make every realm of opportunity for you come subject to my voice." While God speaks in invisible realms, it is important to recognize that He is sending you messages in this same realm. Your spiritual ear must be keen to hear the Father at all times, strategically positioned to make war.

While God speaks in invisible realms, it is important to recognize that He is sending you messages in this same realm.

Come subject to God's voice is a command that Sennacherib, king of Assyria, had to obey in 2 Chronicles 32. Remember, an external dare comes from an outside source. *"Sennacherib king of Assyria came, and entered into Judah, and encamped against the fenced cities, and thought to win them for himself," verse 1. "And when Hezekiah saw that Sennacherib was come, and that he was purposed to fight against Jerusalem, He took counsel with his princes and his mighty men to stop the waters of the fountains which were without the city: and they did help him," verse 2 and 3.*

When the enemy is bold enough to come into your territory and declare war, your FAITH should go into overdrive. It's certainly not going down like this! Hezekiah, king of Judah, understood several things about being strategically positioned to win the challenge:

1. The enemy is in the wrong place: on our territory.
2. I will not give the enemy our resources (water) to help them win the war.
3. I need help!

Recognizing where the enemy is positioned, what He is doing, and how He plans to carry out His strategy against you is a vantage point you must have in order to win. Being cognizant of this will better position you for the challenge. Hezekiah saw what king Sennacherib was trying to accomplish and took immediate action. NEVER give the enemy time to re-strategize and carry out His plan against you or the resources to do it.

Lastly, you need help in defeating your enemy. Although Hezekiah was the king, he understood he couldn't be a lone ranger. You need someone to help you conquer obstacles that come against you. Remain in the posture of prayer, and God will send the necessary help you need to defeat the enemies of doubt, unbelief, procrastination, and lack of resources. Your strategic position of faith in God will cause you to triumph. Dare to believe.

God will not only give you the wherewithal to conquer the enemy concerning spiritual positioning. He will also show you in the natural world exactly how to circumvent the enemy's plan and position you to help bring your vision to pass. God used the prophet Habakkuk to pen this writing and help guide those who are attentive to His instructional voice in chapter 2. *"And the Lord answered me, and said, Write the vision, and make it plan upon tables, that he may run that readeth it. For the vision is yet for an appointed time, but at the end it shall speak, and not lie: though it tarry, wait for it; because it will surely come, it will not tarry," verses 2–3.* Translated, the previous verses convey the following simple strategic outline:

1. Write your vision on paper. To have no plan is a plan to fail.
2. Timing. Your vision is for an appointed time. Chart out when your plan will take place.
3. Action. Your vision will take place if you implement it. Your goals without implementation are just words on a page.

Your goals without implementation are just words on a page.

You must plan to take an active role concerning your destiny, and the timing must be now. Every day that passes is a day lost, never to be seen again. Don't allow the enemy to keep feeding you defeat. Hezekiah had a plan to keep the enemy out of his destiny (as king of Judah), his timing was perfect, and he implemented exactly what God had given him to do. He reigned twenty-nine years in Jerusalem and could not afford to allow the enemy to thwart or abort God's plan for his life or others.

"Also he strengthened himself, and built up all the wall that was broken, and raised it up to the towers, and another wall without, and repaired Mil-lo in the city of David, and made darts and shields in abundance." 2 Chronicles 32:5. Any gray areas, areas of unbelief, weakness, and points of misdirection, misinterpretation, and misinformation must be addressed. Strengthen yourself through the word of God. Look

at your past successes as a point of reference and build up all that is broken. The enemy is challenging you to a fight, so you must be properly positioned to win.

The enemy is challenging you to a fight, so you must be properly positioned to win.

Do whatever is necessary to conquer defeat: pray, fast, make kingdom connections, write the vision on paper, and seek God continually. You will have enemies throughout the entire process challenging you not to be successful. Strategically position yourself using God's blueprint (His word) and follow His exact instructions for your victory. God's placement for your destiny is definite. Remember you are ripe and right where God wants you: strategically positioned in His divine will.

CHAPTER SIX

The Ultimate Challenge—Believe the Promises of God

The next words of Hezekiah to his followers in Jerusalem were so powerful. *"And he set captains of war over the people, and gathered them together to him in the street of the gate of the city, and spake comfortably to them, saying, Be strong and courageous, be not afraid nor dismayed for the king of Assyria, nor for all the multitude that is with him: <u>for there be more with us than with him</u>: With him is an arm of flesh; <u>but with us is the Lord our God to help us, and to fight our battles</u>. And the people rested themselves upon the words of Hezekiah king of Judah,"* verses 6–8. Hezekiah spoke comfort and in confidence to the people he was leading, assuring them of God's supreme authority and power. You must know without a doubt that God is more than the whole world against you. He is there to help you and will fight your battles.

Hezekiah, as king of Judah, understood that there was only ONE true and living God; he believed the promises of God. The first thing he did was open the doors of house of the Lord and repaired them. Next, he tore down all the idols. The king of Assyria served idol gods and boasted about how he utterly destroyed the gods of other nations. *"…for no god of any nation or kingdom was able to deliver his people out of mine hand, and out of the hand of my fathers: how much less shall your God deliver you out of mine hand?"verse 15.* In order to freely and truly believe God regarding your destiny, you must as a leader or follower rededicate your life to Him tearing down every idol that interrupts your relationship with Him.

Verse 19 further describes their blasphemy: *"And they spake against the God of Jerusalem, as against the gods of the people of the earth, which were the work of the hands of man." "Hezekiah the king, and the prophet Isaiah the son of Amoz, prayed and cried to heaven," verse 20. "The effectual prevent prayer of a righteous man availeth much," James 5:16.* Prayer is a key element in defeating your enemy. Cease not to pray. Hezekiah was facing an external dare from the king of Assyria and was sure that God's arrow of deliverance would hit its target dead on. No matter what outside influences try to buffet you, you have to know that God already knows your outcome. *"For I know the thoughts that I think toward you, saith the Lord, thoughts of peace, and not of evil, to give you an expected end," Jeremiah 29:11.*

Here we are given a clear picture of how God will intervene on your behalf if you believe His promises. *"And the Lord sent an angel, which cut off the mighty men of valor, and the leaders and captains of the king of Assyria. So he returned with shame of face to his own land. And when he was come into the house of his god, they that come forth of his own bowels slew him there with the sword,"* 2 Chronicles 32:21. This verse declares that his own children killed him!

The king of Assyria returned to his hometown in shame. Those who challenge you believing you won't be victorious will have to hide their faces because God assuredly will bring your vision to past. The snares they set up for you will ultimately destroy them.

Dare to believe that God has already made you the victor because you are more than a conqueror by Christ Jesus. The Lord will send an angel to stop all of your enemies. Your victory may not come the way you desire it to come, but it will come. Rest assured as it is recorded: *"God is not a man, that he should lie; neither the son of man that he should repent: hath he said, and shall he not do it? Or hath he spoken, and shall he not make it good?" Numbers 23:19.* The immutability of God is stated here. He is utterly different from the human race. People will make you empty promises, but God is the ultimate fulfillment of promise. *"The Lord is not slack concerning his promise, as some men count slackness,"* 2 Peter 2:9.

God has given you an infallible assertion of victorious promises— stand on it. Emphasis is made on the promise through faith. *"Above all, taking the shield of faith, wherewith ye shall be able to quench all the fiery darts of the wicked," Ephesians 6:16.* The shield of faith means taking God at His word by believing His promises. Such trust in God will protect you from doubts induced by Satan.

Romans 4 depicts that the promises of God are realized through faith. Abraham, who against hope believed in hope that his seed should be mighty in the earth, was not weak in faith neither gave thought as to how old he was nor the deadness of Sarah's womb. *"He staggered not at the promise of God through unbelief; but was strong in faith, giving glory to God: And being fully persuaded that, what he had promised, he was also able to perform," verses 20–21.* The promises of God are yea and amen.

We face challenges every day whether great or small. Without these challenges we would not know how capable God the Father really is. He gives us the courage to triumph over external challenges orchestrated by Him. He has provided us with the vital tools of His word through the prayer of promise causing us to be strategically positioned for challenges solicited by Satan and initiated by human will. The external dare that you are facing or will face in the end will cause your faith to mature and bring you to a place of victory every time.

LIFE APPLICATION

1. Some external challenges are orchestrated by God, solicited by Satan, and initiated by human will. You must recognize the difference and know how to handle them through the word of God. Ask yourself, how is this challenge I'm facing going to bring me to a place of prosperity and success? Has this challenge caused me to believe in God, myself, and my destiny? When reflecting on the challenge journal you created, note what successes you obtained and learning curves you made.

2. Are there specific vital tools (i.e., prayer, fasting, people) God has directed your attention to in order to win the challenge? Identify them and use them to your advantage to thwart the enemy's plan.

3. Have you strategically positioned yourself spiritually and naturally through the word of God to conquer the challenge? God's strategy works much better than your own. Seek Him regarding the vision, timing, and necessary action needed for the challenge.

4. Have you taken the ultimate challenge—to believe the promises of God? There are sixty-six books in the Bible of promises concerning your destiny. Believing the promises of God will position you for a guaranteed outcome of victory.

PART II

Internal Dare

༄

*"And God blessed them, and God said unto them, Be fruitful, and mul-
tiply, and replenish the earth, and subdue it: and have dominion over the
fish of the sea, and over the fowl of the air, and over every living thing that
moveth upon the earth."*
GENESIS 1:28

This scripture expresses God's love and care concerning His creation. God blessed them *(male and female)*, bestowing a gift as
well as assigning a function. It gives detail as to what the function of
the male and female that He created should be. That is to be fruitful,
multiply, replenish, subdue, and have dominion. These five verbs of
faith require courage, an internal strength that manifests externally.

God blessed them *(male and female)*, bestowing a gift
as well as assigning a function.

God was conveying the message, Dare to Believe! And He's telling YOU, Dare to Believe! Every goal you have set for yourself can be reached by applying God's original challenge through faith to your model. Model henceforth means calling, idea, or gift. You may even be on a quest to see what your calling is, what gifts do you obtain, or what ideas will work for you. When you release your faith applied to your model, an internal dare has just been relinquished. You're declaring, "I possess the capacity to **procreate, replenish,** and **rule**."

In the previous section, we examined DARE defined as an external force challenging you to perform an action especially as a proof of courage. In this one, we will explore INTERNAL DARE in the context of courage, defined as possessing the inner mental or moral strength to venture, persevere, and withstand danger, fear, or difficulty.

From the beginning God equipped man and woman with the tools they needed to live in the earth: (1) the capacity to procreate and increase, (2) the ability and knowledge to replenish, (3) and the power to rule and govern. These were three powerful charges given to mankind by God. It has been acknowledged that God gave the charge to both male and female. Therefore you cannot use gender as an excuse not to procreate, replenish, and rule.

God has given you a powerfully unrelenting internal drive that keeps you believing. Apostle Paul expressed it this way: *"Brethren, I count not myself to have apprehended: but this one thing I do, forgetting those things which are behind, and reaching forth unto those things which are before, I press toward the mark for the prize of the high calling of God in Christ Jesus," Philippians 3:13–14.* He's saying I haven't attained everything yet, but I'm pressing. I let go of past hurts, failures, and disappointments and stretch toward my future, which is held by Jesus Christ.

There will be formidable situations, mental reminders, and historical scars that will try to hinder and discourage you from accomplishing your goals, visions, and dreams. It is then that you must *believe* and *continue* in spite of fear or difficulty; it is a clear sign that you possess what it takes to overcome adversity (i.e., daring faith). No one was promised life would be all sunshine and no rainy days, but God has promised you the wherewithal to be fruitful, multiply, replenish, subdue, and have dominion according to Genesis 1:28. So take the rain and the sun and begin to procreate, replenish, and rule.

A couple of years ago I began writing songs. Many of them were born out of my experiences and caused me to see life through many lenses. The rain and the sun seemed to create a big blur that caused me to see double and sometimes nothing at all. My future seemed bleak and hopeless. I wasn't sure how to procreate, replenish, or rule.

One day while living in Chicago I was in the mirror combing my hair, and the sun began to shine so bright that it filled my entire residence. I no longer needed the light that was on. I had never before experienced the sun's powerful rays to this extent. I began to sing, "Thank you for the sunshine and rain even for the heartache and pain. Never would have known you were so capable." The light that illuminated my physical residence had turned on an internal light causing me to see my future more clearly. God's presence had come to light my path.

God's presence had come to light my path.

So many days it had rained in my life internally, and I felt like there was nothing left in me to procreate, replenish, or rule. My then six-year-old daughter heard me singing and asked me, "Mommy, why you thank God for the heartache? Mommy, why you thank God for the pain?" I said to her, "Kharis, because I never would have known how capable God really was." She said, "I don't understand." Sometimes we don't understand why we must go through trials, tests, tribulations, and challenges, but without them we wouldn't really appreciate God's love, goodness, and grace or His supreme power. Sometimes the unwarranted challenges help us understand what kind of courage dwells in us from the Almighty God. We then become as a warhorse—a veteran of many struggles, overcoming them through faith and the potent power of Jesus Christ.

You have been blessed by God with the courage and gift to do the impossible. *"I can do all things through Christ which strengtheneth me," Philippians 4:13.* Apostle Paul makes this statement to the Philippians because he'd experience the three charges aforementioned, given by God, in various situations and ever-changing circumstances and could then and only then make such a bold statement of belief. His conversion from persecuting the church to being its most prominent advocate began on the road to Damascus (heavily populated with Christians). Saul (his name before his conversion) had petitioned the high priest to go to Damascus to wreak havoc upon the church, but God had a different plan for his life. In Acts 9 he met God and was blinded at His presence. There were men, real alive witnesses, with Saul who served as testimonials of his transformation. God will have a witness allowing others to see your spiritual and natural transition from the potential to kinetic as you operate in faith.

On this self-driven assignment to antagonize the church, he realized something had changed internally. Three days had passed with no food or drink, and as he entered Damascus, a disciple named Ananias was positioned by God to heal Saul of his physical blindness and he did so. So Saul was filled with the Holy Ghost and was baptized. *"And straightway he preached Christ in the synagogues, that he is the Son of God," verse 20. "But Saul increased the more in strength, and confounded the Jews which dwelt at Damascus, proving that this is very Christ," verse 22.*

Apostle Paul was one of the greatest and most effective post-era disciples of Jesus Christ: producing numerous churches, replenishing the earth with a multitude of disciples, using his ability to rule over principalities and power to perform miracles and is accredited with writing a great portion of the New Testament. Apostle Paul dared to believe. He internalized and applied the five verbs of faith described in Genesis 1:28 and saw his model work for him repeatedly. You may be on a road that seems dim, but when the light of Jesus Christ illuminates the way, your spiritual eyes will be opened to the fact that you possess the mental or moral strength to venture, persevere, and withstand danger, fear, or difficulty to procreate, replenish, and rule. Get ready to see the manifestation of your faith bring your model to life. Dare to believe!

CHAPTER SEVEN

Capacity to Procreate and Increase

"Be fruitful and multiply" means productive or conducive to producing in abundance. Abundance—meaning beyond the need and into the *overflow*. Dare to be fertile—producing abundantly. You possess the mental and moral strength to produce abundantly. You have the capacity to procreate and increase. Apostle Paul speaks to the church at Corinth about planting, watering, and increasing: *"I have planted, Apollos watered; but God gave the increase,"* I Corinthians *3:6.* This process is necessary to reap a great harvest.

Dare to be fertile—producing abundantly.

Do you know someone who is a farmer or know of someone who owns a farm or maybe have visited a farm? That farmer must first decide what kind of seed he/she wants to plant. A seed is defined as the part of a plant from which a new one will grow. Second, the farmer must cultivate the ground before he/she ever plants one seed. Next, he/she must ensure there is a water source to moisten the crop. Then, sow the seed. Finally, the sunlight will give the needed nourishment of light and life to the crop as it germinates in the ground.

In the same way, you must first decide what seed you are going to plant. Your idea, gift, or calling must be alive in you before you can begin to sow it. A dead seed is useless. Next, sow your seed into good ground. You don't want your efforts in planting to be in vain. Then, cultivate your seed of faith through the word of God. *"So then faith cometh by hearing, and hearing by the word of God,"* Romans 10:17. The more you hear God's word, the greater your faith becomes.

Apply the word of God to your seed. It is your job to ensure it is watered daily with consistent use of the word of God. The seed of faith is already in you. The scripture declares God has dealt to every man a measure of faith. Your seed of faith only has to be the size of a mustard seed, which is minute. Your seed doesn't have to be the size of a giant; it just has to be alive and active. Watch it germinate because you have applied your faith. Finally, God will give the increase.

Your seed doesn't have to be the size of a giant; it just has to be alive and active.

There is a designated *season* for sowing; you have to know when that season is. *"To every thing there is a season, and a time to every purpose under the heaven: ... a time to plant, and a time to pluck up that which is planted,"* Ecclesiastes 3:1–2. It takes *time* to plant and the *season* to reap the harvest. If no seeds are put in the ground to grow during planting season, nothing shall be expected during harvest. For some it may be planting season and others it may be harvest time. Wherever you are in the process of producing, make sure you implement the law of abiding in Christ Jesus; you'll be guaranteed a bountiful harvest. Determine in your heart that during your season of planting seeds of righteousness that it will be on good ground so that it may render a hundredfold fruitful return.

As you sow this seed of faith you are preparing your spiritual and natural ground for a bountiful harvest. The overflow is guaranteed to be yours. What are you sowing to? Whatever a person sows, they reap it. For example, if you sow to higher education, growing your business, healthy living, maturing your financial portfolio, and rearing a God-fearing child, that is what you'll reap. On the other hand if you sow to mediocrity, substandard living, illogical thinking, and poor eating habits, that's what you'll reap.

God has designed you to procreate; bring forth or yield a seed that will *bear fruit*. God instituted this natural procreation so that you will live in a place of everlasting seed; thus you are never without a harvest. You may have many models (ideas or gifts) that require you to plant multiple seeds of faith. Remember you possess the courage needed to accomplish the challenge. Whatever the case, everything you need to bear fruit is in you. Again, everything you need to bear fruit, to procreate is IN YOU. It must be alive and active. Herein lies the key to your success in producing God's purposed plan for your life. Pay close attention.

Jesus was speaking to His disciples: *"I am the vine, ye are the branches: He that abideth in me, and I in him, the same bringeth forth much fruit: for without me ye can do nothing," John 15:5.* Jesus defines who He is, who the disciples are, the location of both, the results of following

His order, and the results of disobedience. Adhering to the law of abiding gives you the capacity to produce (abundant fruit). Jesus is saying that He is your direct link to producing your desired fruit and the increase thereof.

Jesus is saying that He is your direct link to producing your desired fruit and the increase thereof.

Jesus explains the cost of not abiding in Him: *"If a man abide not in me, he is cast forth as a branch, and is withered; and men gather them, and cast them into the fire, and they are burned," verse 6.* If you (the branch) do not stay connected to the vine (Jesus Christ), you'll dry up and never produce. Abiding is the key.

He closes His message to the disciples about bearing fruit on this note: *"Ye have not chosen me, but I have chosen you, and ordained you, that ye should go and bring forth fruit, and that your fruit should remain: that whatsoever ye shall ask of the Father in my name, he may give it you," verse 16.*

Jesus has chosen you; you didn't choose Him. It is clear from His statement that Jesus has chosen you for this challenge. He has chosen you to persevere through every difficult moment of seemingly stifled growth. Jesus said He "ordained" you, meaning He has commissioned you by putting His stamp of approval on you as one that abides in Him. In order for your seed to produce, you must follow the blueprint Jesus has left you. Jesus reiterates to the disciples the first charge that God gave man and woman in Genesis to "be fruitful and multiply." Go and bring forth fruit, procreate, and increase, and whatever you ask the Father in Jesus name, He will give it to you because of your obedience.

The power to obtain, lay hold of, apprehend, and produce all comes from God the Creator as aforementioned. *"But thou shalt remember the Lord thy God: for it is he that giveth thee power to get wealth,"* Deuteronomy 8:18. Jesus is the life source of your fruit bearing. *"The fruit of the righteous is a tree of life,"* Proverbs 11:30. Be determined that you will be a tree of life. If you are planting seeds of righteousness, your fruit will reflect that. *"Either make the tree good, and his fruit good; or else make the tree corrupt, and his fruit corrupt: for the tree is known by his fruit,"* Matthew 12:33. The kind of seed you plant will determine what kind of tree you are and the fruit you bear.

"Wherefore by their fruits ye shall know them," Matthew 7:20. Whatever fruit you produce, good or bad, you will be known for it. For example, if you open a bakery and the sweet smell of your cinnamon rolls, apple crisp cobblers, blueberry muffins, marionberry pies, and other pastries escapes into vicinity of the homes and businesses, consumers will come again and again upon experiencing their delightful taste. On the other hand, if you advertise you're the best accountant on the map and upon receiving services many find your credentials don't match your advertisement, you'll be known for it as well. The kind of seeds (faith, patience, purity of heart, time, dedication, and perseverance) you plant will determine the outcome of your harvest.

Whatever you produce, good or bad, you will be known for it.

The kind of spiritual seeds you plant will be reflective of your outcome. Psalm 1:3 depicts a visual for spiritual procreation: *"And he shall be like a tree planted by rivers of water, that bringeth forth his fruit in his season; his leaf also shall not wither; and whatsoever he doeth shall prosper."* If you plant your spiritual tree by the word of God: you will bring forth fruit in your season and not have to worry about it drying up. Whatever you plant is what you'll reap. Sow to fasting, prayer, and daily devotion in the word of God, and you'll reap a harvest of miracles (both natural and spiritual).

Procreation is both natural and supernatural because you are human and spirit. If you follow the principle of abiding, not only will your earthly storehouse produce but your spiritual house as well. Jesus was telling His disciples you will produce spiritual fruit that shall remain. You'll pass on the fruit of life and righteousness from generation to generation. When you pray your prayers will be answered because you abide in the vine, which is Jesus Christ.

When you make a decree, God is there to back you up. He is there to bring your request to pass. Use your spiritual fruit and watch your love, joy, peace, long-suffering, gentleness, goodness, faith, meekness, and temperance bring forth a bountiful harvest, Galatians 5:22. All of the above mentioned fruit of the Spirit is intangible. Jesus was saying feed your spirit man the fruit of the spirit and your natural man will sprout as a result.

Isaiah 55:11 says the word of the Lord shall not return unto Him empty but prosper (produce) what He sent it to do. As a believer, when you apply God's word to your seed, it has no other choice but to produce. Whatever model (natural or supernatural) you are trying to procreate will take courage. David expressed his assertion of this fact as he was aiming to produce a kingdom of righteousness. *"Wait on the Lord: be of good courage, and he shall strengthen thine heart: wait, I say, on the Lord," Ps 27:14.* Waiting in this sense is not standing idle but using your faith and operating in courage not fear.

Since you have sown your seed in good ground in the season that you are suppose to with the law of abiding, now you can *increase* (multiply). If the system of multiplication is in place while you are producing, you won't have to reinvent the wheel, doing your first works over again. Your seed should forecast next year's harvest. For example, if in an agrarian economy a farmer prepares the ground and seed for the next season of harvest, he/she will experience gain again and again instead of a deficit. Prepare for increase by cultivating your seed. What do you want to produce and see increase over time? Are you thinking of starting a new business? Developing new youth programs to help your community? Expecting your first child? Saving for the next investment property? The link between procreation and increase is preparation and cultivation.

The link between procreation and increase is preparation and cultivation.

People look forward to an increase during their career over time. No one wants to stay at the same salary when it's time for their annual performance review. As the manager examines their areas of performance; punctuality, commitment, effort and so forth he/she is also examining any areas of strengths and improvement. At the end of their review, a decision is made whether their work ethics merit an increase. Preparation for the increase took place several months before their review. Part of the preparation was timeliness, initiative, intuitiveness, perseverance, dedication, endurance and other areas that would affect the increase.

It is much the same concerning your model (idea, gift, or calling) that God has given you. Preparation is a key element that needs to be included in your formula for increase. According to Genesis 6, Noah had to build an ark of gopher wood before he was able to put two of each kind and his family aboard. God had given him precise instructions regarding how the ark should be built. *"And this is the fashion which thou shalt make it of: The length of the ark shall be three hundred cubits, the breath of it fifty cubits, and the height of it thirty cubits," Genesis 6:15.*

"By faith Noah, being warned of God of things not seen as yet, moved with fear, prepared an ark to the saving of his house; by the which he condemned the world, and became heir of the righteousness which is by faith," Hebrews 11:7. Granted, Noah had never seen rain, but at the word of his Creator, he prepared for it. You may have some amazingly incredible goals that are on unfamiliar territory. Don't be afraid of succeeding; just prepare for your season. Then, when opportunity knocks you will be ready.

If you are ill prepared for the next step of growth, it is highly likely there will be none. It's called stunted growth. God was about to eliminate everything in the earth except for Noah, the seven who were with him, and the animals He'd chosen to spare. Increase was about to take place in Noah's life and in the lives of others, but preparation and obedience were necessary. Noah had to have courage—the mental or moral strength to venture, preserve, and withstand danger, fear, or difficulty to experience increase. In total, there were eight people that God was giving a new beginning, and you are a product of that number.

God Almighty has given you an idea, plan, project, gifts, and talents to bring multiplication into your world (way of living). It's time to divorce fear and marry courage.

Dare to believe God.

"Prove me now herewith, saith the Lord of hosts, if I will not open you the windows of heaven, and pour you out a blessing, that there shall not be room enough to receive it," Malachi 3:10. *"A man's gift maketh room for him, and bringeth him before great men,"* Proverbs 18:16. Don't wait on validation from others who aren't seeing your model as God does. *"Every good gift and every perfect gift is from above,"* James 1:17. God will surround you with "great men" who will appreciate your gifts and talents, and they will assist you in your areas (if any) of needed growth.

"A man's gift maketh room for him, and bringeth him before great men."

Look at the parable of the talents found in Matthew 14. There was a man who was travelling into a far country and called his servants and gave them goods. *"And unto one he gave five talents, to another two, and to another one; to every man according to his own ability; and straightway took his journey,"* verse 15. *"After a long time the lord of those servants cometh, and settled accounts with them," verse 19.* The one whom he gave five talents increased by five, the one whom he gave two talents increased by two, and the one whom he gave one talent buried his.

They all had the same amount of *time to increase* according to their own ability. The latter of the three made a decision not to prepare for his lord's return by failing to cultivate his gift. Don't be as this servant was and fail to devote time and thought, refinement, bestow attention, care, and labor upon, with a *view of valuable returns* to your model (gift, talent, or calling). You have the time and ability to look through the lens of cultivation dedicating yourself to consistency and possibilities. God will do the rest. If you are willing to put forth every effort to believe, God will help you through preparedness and cultivation. No good thing will He withhold from you. Get ready to see increase in your life; it will become the norm. Increase the value of your life daily; dare to prepare and cultivate your future.

CHAPTER EIGHT

Ability and Knowledge to Replenish

Usually an individual is hired at a certain salary range according to his or her ability and knowledge to manage the job description (challenge) given. Ability—the quality of being able to do something, especially the physical, mental, financial, or legal power to accomplish something. Knowledge—acquaintance with facts, awareness, truths, principles, or understanding gained through experience, investigation, or study. Coupled, having the ability and knowledge positions and empowers the individual to ask for a salary range that is within his or her scope of experience.

In some cases there are duties outside of the job description that falls under the said position. These duties must be fulfilled as part of the unwritten but stated job description. The person's education and experience are part of the evaluation process in determining if he or she is the right fit for the position. These qualifications sometimes affect the ability to manage the said responsibilities outside of the scope of the job description.

Along with references and what the resume states, the candidate is sometimes given a placement or knowledge test to see if he or she has the propensity to produce capital gain. If so, that person would likely be hired rather than his or her counterpart who did not possess these attributes. Although this position may have been filled by a previous employee, this particular candidate is chosen for the *first time* to fill this open position. If it is found that the selected candidate has the potential to replenish and marginalize company interests over time, he or she is acknowledged as an asset and promoted.

It is with this thought that mankind has been selected by God among all the creatures of the earth to replenish having the ability and knowledge to do so.

God told Adam and Eve to "replenish the earth" because He'd given them the ability and knowledge to do so. Everything they needed to be "hired" for the job was already in them. They didn't have to take a placement or knowledge test to see "if." There was no "if" factor because they were made in the image and after the likeness of God according to Genesis 1:26. And in His image and likeness is ability and knowledge. You are not a candidate waiting for the vote of others to elect you to fill, make full, or complete anything. God the Father has given you the ability and the authority to replenish the earth.

God already knew when He gave the charge to man and woman in Genesis 1 to "replenish the earth" that they could and would. Man and woman began to *fill the earth for the first time* when Adam knew his wife Eve and she conceived and bore Cain and his brother Abel, thus "the first family." Children were born unto them and their children's children from generation to generation. Jesus Christ came through forty-two generations of replenishing by God's supernatural interception of the highly favored Virgin Mary. Not only does mankind possess the ability to replenish through physical reproduction but by natural succession as well.

Jesus Christ came through forty-two generations of replenishing by God's supernatural interception of the highly favored Virgin Mary.

This may be your first time implementing your idea, acting on your calling, developing a new business or practice, pursing a potential mate, or using your gift. Don't act in fear. Be bold and confident. God has given you the ability and knowledge to replenish, pursue, and obtain. Dare to believe.

God formed man and had given him instructions not to eat of the tree of knowledge of good and evil. God further stated in Genesis 2:17, *"thou shalt surely die."* Beguiled by Satan, Adam and Eve ate of the forbidden fruit falling from a state of innocence into a condition characterized by sin. Lying, blame, deceit, murder, and various other adverse character flaws caused by disobedience was now in the earth realm as a result. Because the disobedience and wickedness of mankind was great in the earth and every imagination of the thoughts of his heart was evil continually, God caused a flood to cover the earth, saving Noah and his family only. Then God gave Noah and his sons instructions to fill the earth *again*. After the Flood, the mandate given to mankind is restated. *"And God blessed*

Noah and his sons, and said unto them, Be fruitful, and multiply, and replenish the earth," Genesis 9:1.

Replenish now takes on a new meaning. The initial command to replenish the earth was to fill for the first time. Now God said fill the earth again to replace that which I have destroyed by the flood. "And I will establish my covenant with you; neither shall all flesh be cut off any more by the waters of a flood; neither shall there any more be a flood to destroy the earth," Genesis 9:11. "And the rainbow shall be in the cloud; and I will look upon it, that I may remember the everlasting covenant between God and every living creature of all flesh that is upon the earth," verse 16. God says when you replenish the earth, he will bless what you replenish and will not destroy it by "flood" ever again. Note, as in Genesis 1:28, "God blessed them." God did not remove His blessing from mankind because of the fall of man and his direct disobedience to Him. Instead He displayed love toward what He had created in His image (male and female).

God has given you the ability and knowledge to fill again that which may have been destroyed by the flood of life. Maybe your idea was shot down by unbelieving naysayers. Others may have taken your gift for granted not acknowledging the grandeur of your abilities. Or maybe your business needs an internal and external overhaul to reflect the beauty it obtains. In summation, sometimes you have to replenish what has been diluted, buried, or flooded.

Without replacing or putting back that which has been used in the earth, the earth would become barren. So it is the challenge of the human race to take care of the earth so that it is inhabitable. God put man in the Garden of Eden to dress it and keep it according to Genesis 2:15. God knew when He created the earth, the fullness there of, the world, and they that dwell therein that the people in the earth would need to nurture it in order for it and them to survive. Cohabitation of humans and animals would be necessary for the livelihood of planet earth. The fullness thereof—the sun, moon, stars, other planets, and the heavenly hosts—play their role in helping with the replenishment. The sun, for example, gives the earth light by day, the moon and stars by night.

God's intention surrounding replenishing is ascertained: *"And you, be ye fruitful, and multiply; bring forth abundantly in the earth, and multiply therein," verse 7.* It is documented that replenishing does not come through osmosis, but by a well thought out and executed plan by the Creator Himself. Your ability and knowledge to replenish was intentional, not an accident. On purpose God has given you the awesome challenge to continue during your lifetime to fill your destiny with abundance and overflow.

For example, it is proven if you plant one tomato seed, several will grow on the stalk. The next year during planting season you have to replenish the seed again to reap the harvest again. Nothing will happen without agricultural application. Thereby, it is necessary to continue to replace resources that are not natural. Natural resources like air, forest, mineral deposit, or fresh water that is a part of nature is a necessary part of human existence. You have the ability and knowledge to bring forth abundant fruit in your life because God has given you the natural and supernatural resources necessary to do so.

It is documented that replenishing does not come through osmosis, but by a well thought out and executed plan by the Creator himself.

With the God-given ability and knowledge to replenish the earth and human reproduction, it is then fair to conclude that the law of replenishing works for your model (gift, calling, or idea). Dare to believe that you have the replenishing tools to continue to be successful at living out your dream. Replenishing may be for the *first time* or *again*. Don't stop at one success or accomplishment, but continue until you are in the overflow and are positioned such that you have to share with someone else.

The widow woman in Zarephath according to I Kings 17 had experienced drought along with other neighboring cities. God sent the prophet Elijah to this woman saying, *"Arise get thee to Zarephath which belongeth to Zidon, and dwell there: behold, I have commanded a widow woman there to sustain thee,"* I Kings 17:9. Elijah obeyed the voice of God and went as he was instructed. Upon his arrival he asked the woman for some water and some bread. The woman said to Elijah, *"As the Lord thy God liveth, I have not a cake, but a handful of meal in a barrel, and a little oil in a cruse: and, behold, I am gathering two sticks, that I may go in and dress it for me and my son, that we may eat it, and die,"* I Kings 17:12.

Several things were happening in this story:

1. There was a drought that lasted three years and six months.
2. Elijah the prophet was part of the drought and is sent by God to a widow woman.
3. God said that this woman would provide food for the prophet.
4. She didn't have enough food to last throughout the famine.

God had challenged the prophet to believe His words. Remember dare means to challenge to perform an action especially as a proof of courage. It was certainly going to take courage for Elijah and the widow woman. Listen to what he told her next in verse 13.

"And Elijah said unto her, fear not; go and do as thou hast said: but make me thereof a little cake first, and bring it unto me, and after make for thee and thy son." "And she went and did according to the saying of Elijah: and she, and he, and her house, did eat many days. And the barrel of meal wasted not, neither did the cruse of oil fail, according to the word of the Lord, which he spake by Elijah," verses 15 and 16. Talk about replenishing! Because she dared to believe the words of the prophet who was instructed by God to go to her house, she was able to have plenty to share.

God wants you to experience the overflow. He wants your meal barrows to never run empty and your oil to never dry up. There may be a breach in your barrel and your cruse, but if you are willing to stretch your faith and believe the Almighty God, you will experience overflow in the time of drought. Don't allow what you see to distract you from your time of replenishing. It may look like you are down to your last, but when you give God the *first of the last,* it will become everlasting.

God wants you to experience the overflow.

The widow woman gave Elijah the first cake. Are you willing to give God your first? The first fruits of your increase, this may include prayer and meditation, tithes and offering, talents and gifts, and the fruit of your lips, offering praise unto Him. These actual events of Elijah and the widow woman allow us to take a closer look at ourselves and examine:

1. Are we experiencing drought? If so, in what area of our lives?
2. Have we considered that the drought can come to an end through obedience?
3. Are we willing to step out of fear into faith and allow replenishing to take place?
4. Are we willing to share the abundance with others?

The widow woman seemed to be positioned in a state of drought and would end her story in death. But God looked on the affliction of her and her son sending their arrow of deliverance in the form of the prophet Elijah. Not only was the widow woman and her son sustained but the prophet as well. You will not always be in the same position you are in now.

For example, ten years ago you probably weren't at the same job you are now, have the same career choice, car, housing, friends, eating habits, and so forth. They were replaced with something/someone else giving way to growth, stability, and new information. Time brings about knowledge. Having the knowledge that you could replenish has brought you to a state of knowing what worked, what didn't, and what could work regarding your plan for your future. You have the innate ability to replenish your destiny consistently. Don't let your creativity to replenish your dreams and vision die; believe that God will sustain you in the time of drought.

CHAPTER NINE

Power to Rule and Govern

*D*unamis, a Greek term for power, is the ability or strength with which one is endued and exercises. Jesus spoke to the seventy that He sent out to preach the gospel and said upon their return *"Behold I give unto you power to tread on serpents and scorpions, and over all the power of the enemy: and nothing shall by any means hurt you," Luke 10:19.* Your power is universally recognized by satanic governments and carries the signature of the blood of Jesus Christ; therefore you must administer the regulations set forth in His word.

In the same way, a judge is given administrative power by the official government to conduct judicial business governing local, district, or state levels concerning policies and procedures. It is therefore universally accepted in a court of law the ruling of such a judge because he/she has been endowed with this authority. If a person wishes to pursue another verdict, he or she may, in some cases, have the right to petition the Supreme Court for a hearing which is the highest federal court in the United States, consisting of nine justices and having jurisdiction over all other courts in the nation.

You possess supreme power through Jesus Christ to rule and govern your destiny. You have the power to operate without fear of failing, lack of confidence, and resources. Jesus is saying, "Dare to Believe." He's also saying He gives you the courage—mental or moral strength to venture, preserve, and withstand danger, fear, or difficulty. This statement of fact concerning power was not just to the seventy but to every believer, including you, who decides to possess and operate in the authority given to him or her.

Let's dissect this verse. Behold (look, pay attention) I (your Creator) give unto (turn over possession of) you (as an individual) power (authority) to tread (press or step on) serpents and scorpions (venomous poison) and over all the power of the enemy (everything that tries to hinder your progress) and nothing (no thing) shall by any means (source or power) hurt (bring harm) you (your person, property, livelihood, or spiritual growth). Translated: look, pay attention, as your Creator I give authority to you to press on or step on venomous poisons that try to hinder your progress and no thing by any source or power can bring harm to your person, property, livelihood, or spiritual growth.

Venomous poisons can be distractions, detours, misnomers, unpredictable circumstances, dominions, powers, and realms that come to deplete you of your energy and authority to rule and govern your destiny. Don't be afraid of success. To be able to have dominion over your future is to have peace. If you know you can control, to a certain extent, your destiny, by applying Godly principles you'll alleviate an incredible amount of stress from your life. You have been given the supreme authority by Jesus Christ to regulate dominions, principalities, and realms.

Don't be afraid of success.

The power to rule and govern is not only given by election as with a judge but sometimes given by monarch. You are a hereditary ruler because you are in the lineage of the omnipotent Jesus Christ. He is all-powerful and gives authority to the believer. If you dare to believe in Jesus Christ and humble yourself under His mighty hand, you are promised to experience Kingdom authority here on earth and eternal reign in heaven. Here is a detailed description of who you are in Christ Jesus, *"But ye are a chosen generation, a royal priesthood, a holy nation, a peculiar people,"* I Peter 2:9.

There were several "chosen" great people in the Bible that ruled and governed their affairs and the affairs of others that made historical markers. Deborah the prophetess the fifth and only female judge summoned Barak and told him it was God's will that he lead her forces against the mighty warrior, Sisera. Barak, who requested the presence of Deborah to come with him and other soldiers to the war, won a courageous battle leaving no man alive. Samuel, the last judge, anointed David as king. David the second king of Judah and Israel led a dynasty directly to Jesus Christ Himself. Solomon, David's successor, ruled well with the wisdom endowed to him by God, built a temple for God fashioned with doors made of pure gold and the veil of blue, purple, crimson, and fine linen. You have been ordained by God to live a life in kingdom authority and leave a legacy for generations to come.

It is without question that He is the supreme God that has given you the same power to rule and govern your daily life. He wants you to stop questioning whether you have power and begin to operate in it. He left you an instruction manual (the Bible) to guide you as to how to exercise your right as a believer to kingdom benefits. You have a certain allotment of time given by God to reign within your region, scope, and ability; rule well. *"Let the elders that rule well be counted worthy of double honor, especially they who labor in the word and doctrine,"* I Timothy 5:17.

One of the most powerful benefits and tools God has given you as a believer is your ability to speak. You cannot rule or govern your destiny without speaking it into existence. As royal heirs in the kingdom of Jesus Christ you have been given power to speak prosperity, wholeness, victory, favor, peace, and righteousness. *"Death and life are in the power of the tongue: and they that love it shall eat the fruit thereof,"* Proverbs 18:21. God has given you the ability to govern proclamations. Always speak life so that the fruit of what you say will bring abundance instead of damnation.

Jesus said, *"for out of the abundance of the heart the mouth speaketh,"* Matthew 12:34. It is apparent that there is a direct correlation of the heart and what comes out of the mouth. When you are of a pure heart, God will send great abundance to you and even those who dwell with you. You must avidly speak those things that are not as though they already are. Utilize your kingdom authority to change the course of your destiny; internally you'll dare to believe over and over and you won't regret it.

LIFE APPLICATION

1. INTERNAL DARE has been used in this section in the context of courage, defined as possessing the inner mental or moral strength to venture, persevere, and withstand danger, fear, or difficulty. Do you possess these qualities? Are you able to withstand the challenges that you may face throughout life? You have been given tools for such challenges. Apply them to your situations.

2. God set forth a challenge to mankind to be fruitful, multiply, replenish, subdue, and have dominion in the book of the beginning. Are these verbs of faith manifesting in your life? Can you see the tangible and intangible results of daring to believe God?

3. You have read the passages on: capacity to procreate and increase, ability and knowledge to replenish, and power to rule and govern. Are you prepared to produce at the rate of multiplicity not addition, replenishing your model as needed to rule and govern your destiny as God planned from the beginning?

PART III

Faith

"The just shall live by faith."

ROMANS 1:17

I heard these words throughout my childhood. Who is the "just" and what is "faith" I'd wonder?

I later understood that the "just" were those individuals who chose to live their lives according to the word of God. And "faith" was to the *just* acting on the word of God.

There are some things that God has given me to share with you in this part that I believe are relevant to where you may be in your faith walk. To some it may hit home now, and for others it may be significant later. Your belief in God has a direct affect on goal setting and reaching, how quickly you obtain them, and how relevant they are to the times we live in.

This chapter will define faith; explore the different characteristics of faith, the uses of faith, and how it affects your daily life. We will look at just a snapshot of faith because the depth is too great to be encompassed in this brief section.

As we look at faith and view some of its characteristics, we will see that it: (1) has valid content (extremely powerful as it is spoken in words), (2) has a valid object (i.e., God), (3) has a purpose (move with intended direction), and (4) produces works (prompting miracles) causing God to act on your behalf. Faith can be utilized in different areas of your life: to obtain tangible (physical) and intangible (non-physical) goals. Faith affects your daily life and how you respond to things in your sphere. You must be cognizant of your faith frequency, pitch, and tone so that you don't miss the *sound* of success that God wants you *tuned* in to.

We've discussed DARE at length in the previous two chapters, external and internal. Recall, an *external dare* means to challenge to perform an action, especially as a proof of courage. An *internal dare* is used in the context of courage, defined as possessing the mental or moral strength to venture, persevere, and withstand danger, fear, or difficulty.

Thus, Dare to Believe—accepting the challenge to attain your goals, living out your purpose, and persevering through fear or difficulty streamlining your faith in God.

At this section's core lies one objective: to provoke you to unlock and unleash your faith and embrace the fulfillment of your dreams *every day*. Even God took the necessary time to create the world and human existence. You too must exercise patience through the process of perfection. Faith and fulfillment work in concert with one another. It is only when you grasp this concept in the pages of your mind that you will experience God's perfect plan for your life.

You too must exercise patience through the process of perfection.

The word *faith* is mentioned in the Bible nearly three hundred times. Its significance to God must be extremely high. *"But without faith it is impossible to please him..." Hebrews 11:6.* To believers faith is like water to a fish; they can't live without it. Faith is part of the Christian life from the beginning to the end. The believers' foundation is founded upon this theology. Your objective should be to please God daily. You please God when you utilize your faith. Faith is the constant that keeps you living day by day. It breathes life into your existence: physically, emotionally, mentally, spiritually, and I dare not forget to mention financially.

"Through faith we understand that the worlds were framed by the word of God, so that things which are seen were not made of things which do appear," Hebrews 11:3. There was nothing, God spoke and it was so: the solar system, day and night, the waters, the wind, mammals; the entire cosmos. He is the genius behind what you see. *"The earth is the Lord's, the fullness thereof; the world, and they that dwell therein," Psalms 24:1.* All things (heaven, earth, things visible and invisible) were made by God, and without Him nothing was made, John 1:3.

This includes Gods skillful design of mankind. God created man in His image, formed him from the dust of the ground (corporeal part of mankind), and breathed into his nostrils the breath of life (incorporeal part of mankind) *"and man became a living soul," Genesis 2:7.* The soul (will, intellect, and emotions) is the part of you that is life. It is important to establish that the soul directly correlates with faith because the soul is the core of human existence. It is your communication line to God. A body with no soul is merely a corpse. Adam was dead when God formed him. It wasn't until God breathed into his nostrils that Adam received life. The word "breath" in Genesis 2:7 is the Hebrew word *ruach*, which means spirit. Faith is dead (without spirit) with no works: the dead does not work. Thus, at the inception of His creative wonders, *"God dealt to every man the measure of faith," Romans 12:3.* God created you with inborn faith.

The ability to be able to believe distinguishes you from any other life form that God has created. The creatures in the heavens above, the earth below, and in the sea beneath depend solely on the *grace* of God for their provision. Yes, they are conscious of their need to feed and house their young, but they do not obtain the *understanding* that God their Creator is the one that provides for them. Neither has God the Father of all creation given to them the awareness of *belief* in Him.

Since you were made in His image and *made little lower than the angels,* you are cognizant of your existence and must at the same time enact your knowledge of God, thereby using your faith, Psalm 8:5. Your state of consciousness, deductive reasoning, and humanness grants you faith. Even an infant understands if he can communicate in some form he will get what he needs from his caretaker—that's faith. Every time you say, "I'm going to..." you activate your faith. When you speak your destiny, you release a power within that prompts movement in an invisible realm that's incredibly and amazingly undeniable.

"Dare to Believe" encapsulates seeking to prove by quest fulfilled destiny, using your untapped potential through faith. When you DARE to believe, you open the gateway to so many possibilities.

Your faith can be utilized in many ways—to gain eternal life and a crown of righteous, soul winning and disciplining others, miracles of physical, mental, emotional, financial, and spiritual healing, career growth, build Godly family structure and principles just to mention a few. Let's delve into faith with the intent of defining, characterizing, and utilizing it to explore untapped potential and unveil internal hope.

CHAPTER TEN

Faith Defined

"*Now faith is the substance of things hoped for the evidence of things not seen,*" *Hebrews 11:1.* Faith is an intangible unquestioning belief. You cannot physically touch it; you cannot see it with the human eye, and it cannot be reasoned by metaphysical laws. Faith is defined as a belief or confident attitude toward God, involving commitment to His will for one's life. It is a spiritual gift from the Creator that He has "*dealt to every man the measure*" as recorded in Romans 12:3. God has given each believer tailor-made gifts and an amount (measure) of those gifts that enables him/her to do what He has challenged him/her to do and get the expected outcome.

The result of faith's manifestation is its operation. Dormant faith yields no results. "*Faith without works is dead being alone,*" *James 2:17.* "*Yea, a man may say, thou hast faith, and I have works: show me thy faith without thy works, and I will show thee my faith by my works,*" *Verse 18.* In other words you can say you have faith, but nothing will happen if you don't activate it. Active faith causes God to move on your behalf. It takes courage to use faith.

Dormant faith yields no results.

Courage is active. When you have the mental or moral strength to persevere against difficulty and danger, you operate in a realm that many are afraid to. God has then identified you as a candidate of faith. What happens is the measure in which God has distributed to you is being tested. He will see if you utilize what He has given you to increase the measure.

Faith is not founded on fear; it does not submit to weakness, neither does it bow to impossibilities. *"But without Faith it is impossible to please him: for he that cometh to God must believe that he is, and that he is a rewarder of them that diligently seek him," Hebrews 11:6.* Your faith in operation pleases God. When you petition God for something, you must believe that He is God and that your prayer will be answered as you seek Him. The following account of faith clearly expresses an example of courage mixed with the measure of faith.

Your faith in operation pleases God.

In Mark 9 a father had a son who had a dumb and deaf spirit. He brought him to the disciples to be healed, but they could not because of their lack of faith. Jesus said to the disciples in verse 19, *"O faithless generation, how long shall I be with you? how long shall I suffer you? bring him unto me."*

Jesus asked the father how long it had been since his son had this tormenting spirit. The father answered since he was a child. It is paramount to mention the time. It is evident that now the son is no longer a child. Jesus said unto the father, *"if thou canst believe, all things are possible to him that believeth," verse 23. "And straightway the father of the child cried out, and said with tears, Lord, I believe; help thou mine unbelief," verse 24.* The father expressed grief and told Jesus he'd had to see his son tormented by throwing himself into the fire and water for several years because of this foul spirit; please help his unbelief.

Sometimes you can believe God for something, and after a period of time has passed and it hasn't manifested, you may become discouraged. Do as this father did and ask God to help your unbelief. The father had the courage to bring his son to Jesus *even after* the disciples could not heal him. He also had a measure of faith that prompted Jesus to respond to his petition. Do not allow your first attempt of not receiving an answer to your petition stifle your faith. Jesus responds to consistent and persistent faith.

As with the Canaanite woman whose faith was tested, her daughter was grievously vexed with a devil in Matthew 15:21–28. The woman, a Gentile, besought Jesus on behalf of her daughter to be healed. Jesus told her that He was sent to the *"lost sheep of the house of Israel (Jews),"* testing her faith. Again she came to Jesus and said, *"Lord, help me."* He answered and said, *"It is not meet to take the children's bread, and to cast it to the dogs." "And she said, Truth, Lord: yet the dogs eat of the crumbs which fall from their masters' table."* The woman was saying, "I know I'm not a Jew, but what you have I'm in need of and my faith tells me I'm going to receive it."

The woman was consistent and persistent with her request. Although it seemed as if Jesus was not going to answer her petition because of His answers, she still pressed in faith on behalf of her daughter. Are you willing to press in to Jesus on someone else's behalf? Faith is unselfish. Jesus answered, *"O woman, **great is thy faith: be it unto thee even as thou wilt. And her daughter was made whole from that very hour,"* verse 28.* Your faith will be tested, but you must with consistency and persistency seek out an answer from God.

Faith is unselfish.

The father in Mark 9 sought out an answer from Jesus. He responded to the father's faith and *"rebuked the foul spirit, saying unto him, Thou dumb and deaf spirit, I charge thee, come out of him, and enter no more into him. And the spirit cried, and rent him sore, and came out of him,"* verses 25 and 26.

The disciples asked why they couldn't cast out the spirit, and Jesus answered them saying this kind of spirit can come out only by prayer and fasting. Some petitions will take *prayer, faith, and fasting* to get God to respond. Note the woman (a Gentile) with the daughter vexed with the devil had "great faith," and Jesus called the disciples (Jews) a "faithless generation." Where are you positioned on the continuum of faith—great faith or faithless?

CHAPTER ELEVEN

The Prayer of Faith

Faith must have a valid content. What do the words you speak to God contain? Do they have meaning? The prayer of faith is your direct two-way communication line to God. Prayer is simply talking to God and God to you. What you say to God is important. *"Be careful for nothing; but in every thing by prayer and supplication with thanksgiving let your requests be made known unto God," Philippians 4:6.*

Prayer is also used so that God can speak to you concerning His will and plan for your life. It gives you the internal connection with God deepening and strengthening your relationship with Him. The prayer of faith is a powerful tool used to speak to invisible realms pulling down strongholds, causing direct change, and prompting God to answer you.

Jesus said, *"men ought always to pray, and not to faint," Luke 18:1.* Jesus prayed throughout His ministry on earth. The following are just a few: when He turned water into wine, when He fed the five thousand, three times in the garden of Gethsemane before His betrayal of Judas—note this prayer was different from any Jesus had prayed before. *"And being in agony he prayed more earnestly: and his sweat was as it were great drops of blood falling to the ground," Luke 22:44.* Sweat as great drops of blood! This was an intense prayer, one that reflected total focus, meaning, and passion. How intense are your prayers of faith? This prayer of faith dealt directly with the sin bearer for all mankind for all ages. Jesus was about to be offered up as the sacrifice for the entire human race. Jesus also prayed before He raised Lazarus who had been dead for four days.

"Then they took away the stone from the place where the dead was laid. And Jesus lifted up his eyes, and said, Father, I thank thee that thou hast heard me. And I knew that thou hearest me always: but because of the people which stand by I said it, that they may believe that thou hast sent me," John 11:41–42. Jesus called forth Lazarus out of the grave and said, *"loose him, and let him go."*

Let's dig deeper and dissect what this text shows us. First, they took away the stone, representing a barrier. There may be various sorts of barriers that may try to keep you from reaching God through prayer. When you have identified them, remove them. Then, identify the place where dead communication may reside. Initiate conversation with God as did Jesus when he said, *"Father, I thank thee that thou hast heard me."* "Father" indicted that there was relationship. Jesus was confident that God had heard Him. God is waiting on you. He never sleeps nor slumbers. Jesus said the prayer aloud so that those who were watching to see what happened would believe. Sometimes you may have to verbalize your prayers of faith so that others can believe. Dare to believe in your own prayers.

"And the prayer of faith shall save the sick, and the Lord shall raise him up; and if he have committed sins, they shall be forgiven him," James 5:15. Jesus prayed the prayer of faith believing in God the Father and knowing that the Father heard His prayer and would answer it. His prayer was answered when Jesus called forth Lazarus out of the grave. The prayer of faith discerns God's will and perseveres until it is accomplished.

The prayer of faith discerns God's will and perseveres until it is accomplished.

It is paramount to show that relationship with God is the key to getting your prayers answered. What does your relationship with God look like? Is it faint or strong? Does He know your voice? When you have relationship with someone, that person's voice becomes familiar to you. You can hear it in a distance, recognizing it among many others, and know who it is even if he or she is showing extreme emotions of joy or tears because relationship has been established. That is how you want your prayers (voice) to be to God. You want Him to recognize your voice among all the prayers that He hears.

God recognized Jesus's voice and knew it was Jesus talking to Him. If Jesus had to pray to the Father and He is the Christ, how about you? Your prayer of faith will change the course of your destiny, bring food where there is scarcity, take what you have and turn it into what you need, command God's will to be done in your life, and resurrect dead situations and people. The prayer of faith will cause impossible situations to become possible realms of manifestation.

Daniel prayed to God three times a day, and the Father acknowledge his prayers. King Darius put Daniel in the lions' den for disobeying his decree to not pray for thirty days. Imagine not being able to pray for thirty days! God came to his rescue: *"My God hath sent his angel, and hath shut the lions' mouths, that they have not hurt me: forasmuch as before him innocence was found in me; and also before thee, O king, have I done no hurt,"* Daniel 6:22.

Be assured that your prayer of faith will cause God to send angels to shut the mouths of lions (those that come to devour your faith through unbelief). The king then released him from the lions' den and made a decree that in every dominion of his kingdom men would fear the God of Daniel. He also commanded those who plotted against Daniel, their wives, and their children to be put in the lions' den. Daniel prospered in the reign of Darius and Cyrus the Great. The prayer of faith will change the course of your destiny and promote you. Note that in both instances of Jesus raising Lazarus from the dead and Daniel being freed from the lions' den with no harm, people believed in God as a result. Are you prayers of faith causing others to believe in the Father?

CHAPTER TWELVE

Faith to Inherit Eternal Life

Faith must have a valid object. Faith—a belief in or confident attitude toward God, involving commitment to His will for one's life. The object is God, the giver of eternal life.

As I developed my relationship with God, I began to understand that I was the just, and faith was my belief in Him. I am an adherent of Christ, a Christian, one who believes that He died for my sins and I am now redeemed unto God.

In Mark 11:22, Jesus said four words to the disciples concerning faith: *"Have faith in God."* He didn't say in man, objects, the constellations, or any of the like. He continued in verses 23–24 saying, *"For verily I say unto you, That whosoever shall say unto this mountain, Be thou removed, and be thou cast into the sea; and shall not doubt in his heart, but shall believe that those things which he saith shall come to pass; he shall have whatsoever he saith. Therefore I say unto you, What things soever ye desire, when ye pray, believe that ye receive them, and ye shall have them." James 4:2 says, "Ye have not, because ye ask not."*

This text is loaded with faith! Jesus gave them some instructions on getting their prayers answered by God. He said speak to the mountain by faith. Jesus was not speaking of natural mountains as in Mount Hood or Mount Everest. He spoke of internal mountains the inward things that need to be removed for you to receive from God—mountain being interpreted as the thing that seems too big, too great, overwhelming, and impossible for you to move. There may be situations in your life that keep piling on top of one another—a bad marriage, rebellious child, sick parent, or financial distress, layer upon layer. Speak to it. Tell it to go to a place far from your habitation and drown. Drown means to die. Don't doubt in your heart—it is the place of your decision making. Believe what you say when you pray. It shall come to pass. There is no need of praying if you don't believe.

"Ye ask, and receive not, because ye ask amiss," James 4:3. Never pray vain babblings, wrong, and misdirected prayers. It's just like someone asking you for something, and it sounds like gibberish; you can't understand their request because their heart is not conveying the right speech. When you talk to God about your petition, be clear about what you're asking and that it is according to His will.

When you talk to God about your petition, be clear about what you're asking and that it is according to His will.

Jesus told Thomas in order to inherit eternal (without end) life you must believe in His life, death, resurrection, and ascension. This should be your ultimate goal as a believer. This is one of the most important expressions of faith an individual could have. You can believe God for everything, but if it doesn't include eternal life, everything means nothing. Look at what Jesus had to say about it.

He was talking to the rich young ruler in Matthew 19 who asked, *"Good Master, what good thing shall I do, that I may have eternal life?"* Jesus responded, *"If thou wilt be perfect, go and sell that thou hast, and give to the poor, and thou shalt have treasure in heaven: and come and follow me," verse 21.* The young man went away sorrowful because he had great possessions. Jesus told the disciples who were in his hearing, "With God all things are possible," verse *21.*

He continued, *"Every one that hath forsaken houses, or brethren, or sisters, or father, or mother, or wife, or children, or lands, for my name's sake shall receive a hundredfold, and shall inherit everlasting life," verse 29.* Jesus was saying as a believer you can inherit eternal life in the kingdom of heaven if you're willing to devote your earthen vessel to him by faith. *"Set your affection on things above, not on things on the earth," Colossians 3:2.*

The Savior was not stating here that He doesn't want you to have wealth, but instead, if you let it, it will hinder you from inheriting an eternal life in heaven. It aligns with the first commandment, *"Thou shalt have no other gods before me," Exodus 20:3. "But seek ye first the kingdom of God, and his righteousness; and all these things shall be added unto you," Matthew 6:33.* If you are willing to submit your lifestyle to Christ, your faith, and dare to walk according to His plan, it will render you unlimited access to your needs on earth and an eternal place in heaven. *"In my Father's house are many mansions, if it were not so, I would have told you. I go to prepare a place for you," John 14:2.*

Jesus does not leave the reader hanging in the balance but gives a description of their eternal residence (Holy Jerusalem) in Revelation 21 through the eyes of John. The light to the city is clear as crystal, great and high walls having twelve foundations garnished with precious stones of jasper, sapphire, chalcedony, topaz, and amethyst to name a few, twelve gates of pearl, the streets are pure gold as transparent glass and the glory of God, and the Lamb is present. Faith to inherit eternal life, where is yours?

CHAPTER THIRTEEN

Faith Unseen

"Seeing is believing," is an idiom first recorded in this form in 1639 that means "only physical or concrete evidence is convincing." Above all of your senses, your sight is most easily deceived; you believe it in preference to any other evidence. Today, use your faith to cross over into the unseen, believing in the invisible realm.

When you were a child did you ever want a special something, a bike, go to Disney World, a big birthday party, or lots of money? You saw it in your mind, believed it in your heart, and had confidence in the promise giver before it even happened. You pictured yourself riding the blue or pink bike with colored reflectors, Mickey Mouse shaking your hand, everyone singing happy birthday and bringing you lots of gifts, and yes, your piggy bank full of money! The key to obtaining that which is in the invisible realm is *seeing* in the invisible realm.

One of the characteristics of faith is that it is unseen; it is an invisible realm of belief. Dare to believe God for that which is unseen and *"calleth those things which be not as though they were," Romans 4:17.* You obtain an unseen power that goes to work on your behalf the moment you activate it. Faith is the ability to command the invisible to be visible. It is the tenacity to face the giant of doubt and bring it down in defeat with the stone of victory. Faith is the answer to your desires, dreams, and visions.

Faith is unseen; it is an invisible realm.

Let's go deeper into the unseen realm and see how it is relative to the natural. Jesus, after His resurrection, appeared unto the disciples, but Thomas was not among them. Now, Jesus was a natural man, lived on the earth, died, and was resurrected by God the Father. He was also divine. Thomas had seen Jesus do mighty miracles, and yet this is what he said, *"Except I shall see in his hands the print of the nails, and put my finger into the print of the nails, and thrust my hand into his side, I will not believe," John 19:25.*

"I will not believe," were the words of one of the twelve disciples. Imagine that! Eight days later Jesus appeared unto them again, and Thomas was with them. *"Then came Jesus, the doors being shut, and stood in the midst, and said, Peace be unto you," verse 26.* Jesus supernaturally, probably for the effect (because of Thomas's doubt), came through shut doors! He could have used a door, but because of the blatant doubt of one who walked with Him and saw the miracles He'd performed, he used His supernatural ability.

"Then saith he to Thomas, Reach thither thy finger, and behold my hands; and reach hither thy hand, and thrust it into my side: and be not faithless, but believing," verse 27. Thomas had to see in order to believe, but Jesus said these words to him, *"Thomas, because thou hast seen me, thou hast believed: blessed are they that have not seen, and yet have believed," verse 29.*

You have not seen Albert Einstein, Thomas Edison, Abraham Lincoln, Harriett Tubman, or Langston Hughes in person, but you believe they lived and walked this earth. They left the physics E=MC2 equation, the light bulb, Emancipation Proclamation in 1863, Underground Railroad escape, and "I, Too," poem on record as evidence that they lived. Why not use that same faith unseen to see your dreams and visions come to pass?

CHAPTER FOURTEEN

Faith to Release Your Dreams and Visions

The definition of *faith* has been established as an intangible invisible unquestioning belief. A dream in the same sense is intangible and invisible and at the same time reflects segments of reality. When you dream, some parts of the dream are familiar and others unfamiliar, and when you awaken you are able to recall some details of the dream. Your consciousness of faith has caused you to dream about what you've believed God for. As a result, your connection that binds the dream to reality is your faith.

Faith to release your dreams and visions encompasses moving the images seen in the invisible realm to visible manifestation. For example, if you desire to develop a state-of-the-art daycare center for newborns through age five, you first see the infants in pink blankets, blue knickerbockers, and socks, smiles of toddlers pulling on your leg, and parents joyfully kissing their little ones as they leave them in your capable care.

You see the people who make the dream a reality and then, the facility, programs, and curriculum to bring the vision into focus.

Before you are able to act on something, the *thought*, *desire*, and *will* must be in place. **Thought** is the processes and content of cognition. **Desire** is to long for strongly. **Will** is the mental faculty by which one deliberately chooses or decides upon a course of action. These three embodiments of treasured systems will make your dream a reality coupled with faith.

Here's another example, dreaming to go on vacation in Hawaii, Fiji Islands, or your most desired vacation spot you have to, one think about the possibility of it happening, two desire to want to go, and three will it to be. So you start with the imagination, what it would be like—warm breeze blowing on your face, hot sand between your toes, and the sound of blue waves of water bringing you a cool sensation and so on. You think of what you'd desire to do once you get there—go for a swim in the ocean, enjoy a tropical drink with an umbrella in the glass and a lime on the side of it, ordering island food you wouldn't usually eat at home, and many other adventure excursions. You began to feel yourself there; your desire increases.

So you plan to make it a reality, and your will causes you to take the next step in planning. You look at specifics about which island you'll visit, availability of your schedule, financial data, if you'll take anyone with you, which airlines will take you there, hotels/resorts, car rental, and many other details that surround your vacation. The belief that you are going on your dream vacation is now beginning to take form because it came from within. You have began to take the thought, desire, and will from within and shape what you've seen, heard and felt into real time by actually doing.

Faith to make your dream a reality encapsulates thought, desire, and will. Your faith will cause you to explore new ventures, expand your horizons, and reach beyond what obstacles reveal. Don't allow dream killers and snatchers into your sanctuary of belief; they will cause you to abort your vision. This is the plight of Satan; rebuke Him and all His followers. Dare to release your dreams and visions through utilization of your faith.

Don't allow dream killers and snatchers into your sanctuary of belief; they will cause you to abort your vision.

If you follow the principles of passion surpassing pessimism your dream will never die but will manifest. **Pessimism** is a state of mind that negatively colors the perception of life, especially with regard to the future. This is a direct opposite of passion. **Passion** is a powerfully strong boundless emotion of enthusiasm. When you apply passion to your dream it releases reality.

God gave the inspiration to the prophet Habakkuk to write this verse of scripture: *"Write the vision, and make it plain upon tables, that he may run that readeth it. For the vision is yet for an appointed time, but at the end it shall speak, and not lie: though it tarry, wait for it; because it will surely come, it will not tarry," Habakkuk 2:2–3.* You must write down your vision, plan, or dream; writing it down will cause you to keep it in the forefront of your mind and on the table of your heart. God will guide and help you through every step of faith.

God has given you dreams about how to start a business, an outreach ministry, and other branches of faith. Don't allow Satan to cause you to procrastinate any longer. Your step of faith will pay off. Look at the disciples who had a fishing business. They were washing their nets (giving up) because they had not caught any fish all night long. Jesus told them, *"Launch out into the deep, and let down your nets for a draught," Luke 5:4.* Jesus was saying get out of the shallow water (safe space) and position yourself where there are many opportunities for growth (the deep).

Simon was partially obedient in that he let down his net. Jesus told him to let down his nets. When God gives you instructions regarding your dreams and visions, obey Him to the letter. As Simon launched out into the deep, he caught a great multitude of fish and his net broke. You don't want to lose what God has blessed you with. Properly prepare for the draught that God is going to release to you. He called for his partners in the other ship for help; both ships began to sink because the catch was so great. Your dreams and visions will be so expansive that you will have to call for your destiny partner and share your overflow.

The *result* of faith is the evidence. The great multitude of fish was the evidence. Going on the dream vacation, starting your book, startup of the day care, beginning the television show, establishing a Bible institute are all *results* of faith. It doesn't matter if you desire to go on a dream vacation or claiming victory over the enemy, the power of your belief within (faith) will manifest (results) when you activate it. DARE to Believe! ANY inward idea can become tangible and change your life as well as those that are waiting on your genius. Your intangible faith is waiting to become a reality to show others the way. Use your faith to release your dreams and visions.

CHAPTER FIFTEEN

Miracles of Faith

Faith must have purpose. One of the purposes of faith is to foster various miracles. Miracles happen as a result of your active faith having a direct aim. A miracle is a supernatural act of God that causes the natural to change its current state. Whatever miracle you are believing God for, expect it to come, without reservations, as you operate in pure faith. It doesn't matter what miracle you're expecting—physical or nonphysical—dare to believe. God responds to your faith.

**A miracle is a supernatural act of God that causes
the natural to change its current state.**

Paul exercised his faith in the 14th chapter of Acts. There was a man at Lystra impotent in his feet, cripple from his mother's womb that had never walked. Paul intently observed him and *perceived that he had the faith to be healed.* Paul *"said with a loud voice, Stand upright on thy feet. And he leaped and walked," verse 10.* Paul spoke the word of faith and commanded restoration to the lame man. You may have been waiting on your miracle for years; your active faith will cause it to happen.

In Mark 5 a woman had an issue of blood for twelve years that caused her to be in agony: seeking restoration from many physicians spending all that she had and did not get better but grew worse. She heard of Jesus, the miracle worker, was near, and pressed behind the crowd of people to reach Him. She said within herself (courage— possessing the mental or moral strength to overcome adversity), *"If I may touch but his clothes, I shall be whole," verse 28.* Her faith was ignited to the point that she was willing to be seen in public in her worse state for she knew her current state was about to change. You must believe against physical evidence of what you see and begin to see in the invisible realm your miracle taking place.

You must believe against physical evidence of what you see and begin to see in the invisible realm your miracle taking place.

Look at what happened as a result of her faith in God. *"And straightway the fountain of her blood was dried up; and she felt in her body that she was healed of that plague," verse 29. And Jesus, immediately knowing in himself that virtue had gone out of him, turned him about in the press, and said, Who touched my clothes?" verse 30.* The woman fell down and worshipped Jesus confessing that it was her. *"And he said unto her, Daughter thy faith hath made thee whole; go in peace, and be whole of thy plague," verse 34.*

Your miracle is not contingent on how long you've been waiting, what your current condition or state is, how many people said they were going to help you and didn't, or what others think of you; it's based on YOUR faith in God. *"According to your faith be it unto you," Matthew 9:29.* Your miracle of faith is waiting on YOU. Note that the woman fell and worship God after she received her miracle. After God grants your miracle remember to give Him praise and thanksgiving.

I remember after I'd given birth to my daughter Kharis, I developed fibroid tumors. They caused me to bleed at will, and my stomach looked as if I was still pregnant. I believed God for my miracle and stood on His word that by His stripes I was healed. I just needed one stripe (for my healing)! While I was waiting to see the doctor, I felt great pressure in my lower abdominal region. I went to the restroom, and out came three egg-sized tumors! This miracle of faith helped me understand that God can heal my body. According to your faith, be it unto you even now.

In Joshua 10:12–14, Joshua exemplifies his faith by talking to God and commands the sun and the moon to stand still while they avenged themselves (children of Israel) upon their enemies (the Amorites). Verse 13 declares the sun stood still and the moon stayed. Now this is powerful: *"And there was no day like that before it or after it, that the Lord hearkened unto the voice of a man: for the Lord fought for Israel," verse 14.*

Several things were taking place. One, Joshua activated his faith by talking to God, and as a result, God responded by giving Israel the victory. Two, the physical limitations of time were changed because Joshua spoke to it. You must speak to the boundaries that keep your faith captive. He couldn't see defeat only victory. Three, as a result of Joshua's prayer to God, the Lord caused the physical dynamics of His creation to be disturbed because of the faith of a believer.

You must speak to the boundaries that keep your faith captive.

Joshua believed a miracle would take place and was in expectation that God would manifest Himself greatly on Israel's behalf. His faith changed the course of time forever! A miracle of this magnitude had to be documented. *"So the sun stood still in the midst of heaven, and hasted not to go down about a whole day," Joshua 10:13.* Think about it, the earth spins on its axis revolving around the sun and the moon revolves around the earth. The earth takes twenty-four hours to spin around on its axis: that means that the sun reflected light on the earth "about a whole day," which would be twenty-four hours. In other words, God stopped time because of Joshua's active faith! Has your belief within caused God to act on your behalf and change the impossible, granting you a notable miracle?

CHAPTER SIXTEEN

Hearing the Word of Faith

As we end the faith segment, my fourth and final point: faith produces works. Paul records *"So then faith cometh by hearing, and hearing by the word of God,"* Romans 10:17. Your faith comes about by what you hear, producing works. If you keep speaking and hearing these words: *"Thou shalt lend unto many nations, and thou shalt not borrow,"* Deuteronomy 28:12. *"And the Lord shall make thee the head, and not the tail; and thou shalt be above only, and thou shalt not be beneath,"* Deuteronomy 28:13. *"If you be willing and obedient you'll eat the good of the land,"* Isaiah 1:19. *"Death and life are in the power of the tongue: and they that love it shall eat the fruit thereof,"* Proverbs 18: 21. *"No weapon that is formed against thee shall prosper,"* Isaiah 54:17. *"A man's gift maketh room for him, and bringeth him before great men,"* Proverbs 18:16. All of these statements are demonstratives in your hearing that will prompt your faith to take form and produce.

Dare to believe your faith will work after hearing the word of God and applying it to your model, idea, vision, or dream. Put into practice what you've heard. It will become a part of you. Ever heard "You are what you eat"? Well, you are what you hear. The ear gate is a sensitive instrument used for deciphering information. If what you hear is full of energy and life, that is what you will produce.

The ear gate is a sensitive instrument used for deciphering information.

Imagine you were in a spiritual boot camp for six weeks. Your only daily assignment was to practice the word of God through written exercises, real time hands-on experiments that will effect the next six years of your life and development of future plans that would be intended for the next generation. Your whole way of thinking would change concerning spiritual growth, financial portfolios, family structure, social interaction, mental meditation, and emotional cognitive actions and reactions. This is what should take place on a daily basis as you hear the word of faith.

Surround yourself with like-minded people. *"Be not deceived: evil communications corrupt good manners," I Corinthians 15:33.* In other words bad company corrupts good habits. If the ear hears constant unfruitful nonsensical talk, it will produce just that. You must guard your gateway to thinking (your ear) because it is your lifeline to faith. Whatever your spirit hears is what the body will do, character will become, and vision will see. Ignite your faith through hearing the word of God. It will cause the miraculous to happen for you and generations to come.

You must guard your gateway to thinking (your ear) because it is your lifeline to faith.

LIFE APPLICATION

1. Your faith is the gateway to God the Father. Do you have an understanding of what faith is and how it affects your relationship with God? Your yes or no answer will help guide your future decisions in life.

2. Faith must have a valid content. Do your prayers have meaning? The prayer of faith affects your two-way communication with God. Do you have a strong prayer life? Do you rehearse effectual fervent prayers? Does God know your voice?

3. Your faith must have a valid object (i.e., God). Is God the object of your faith? Explain your answer.

4. Faith must have a purpose. Does your faith have purpose? Your faith can change the direction of your destiny. Apply your faith to every area of your life—healing, finances, spiritual growth, making your dream a reality. Are you willing to stretch beyond your comfort zone of faith and embrace faith unseen?

5. Faith produces works. How often do you hear the word of faith? Every month, week, day? Make a conscious decision to read your Bible, listen to the voice of God, and internalize what is being said to you through various vehicles of faith.

PART IV

Partner with Destiny

"For I know the thoughts that I think toward you, saith the Lord, thoughts of peace, and not of evil, to give you an expected end."

JEREMIAH 29:11

What exactly does "Partner with Destiny" mean? To unite or associate with another or others in an activity, course of events, or sphere of common interest that will inevitably happen in the future. This commonwealth of people assuredly understands that if you institute this action as part of your daily regime you position yourself for endless opportunities without boundaries.

Now that you understand the meaning of Dare from an internal and external perspective and have coupled it with faith, partner with the Kingdom Leader to fulfill your designed purpose here on earth.

Your most valuable partner is God the Creator. If He is habitually part of your daily functionality, you are definitely going to be resilient during difficult times and will ultimately appreciate your commitment to keeping Him as your prime lead partner. Did you hear that "Prime Lead Partner"? Never ever get ahead of God! God has *all* your kingdom connections mapped out and will guide you through each destiny stream if you listen to His incredible plan for ultimate living. Come into agreement with God's word and will for your life.

He knows and understands who you are, how you function, your shortfalls and uprisings, and is most capable of leading you in the path of successful completion of your intended goals. *"Before I formed thee in the belly I knew thee," Jeremiah 1:5.* No one knows like the Father what your fate will render. God will help you in decision making, planning for future ventures, and cultivate the foundation in you that has been formed through His word. God told Jeremiah in verse 9, *"Behold, I have put my words in thy mouth."* And He said, *"I will hasten my word to perform it," verse 12.* Translated, I will watch over my word to ensure it comes to pass in your life. God speaks so clearly regarding his word, *"So shall my word be that goeth forth out of my mouth: it shall not return unto me void, but it shall accomplish that which I please, and it shall prosper in the thing whereto I sent it," Isaiah 55:11.*

God's word is what you should believe and not the devil's lie. Every time Satan tells a lie it is of His own accord. Instead of believing the devil's lie about your destiny, position yourself for kingdom connections, and just wait and see how marvelously things will work in your future.

CHAPTER SEVENTEEN

Don't Believe the Devil's Lie

Satan has lied from the beginning—to God and the angels, exalting Himself to be the supreme God as he took a third of the angels with his tail from Heaven and was cast into the earth, Revelation 12. Satan again lied to the first woman Eve, *"Ye shall not surely die,"* persuading her to eat of her death, Genesis 3:4. To Jesus Christ, with the kiss of betrayal using Judas as His vehicle and to generation after generation and will continue to lie because it is his nature.

When you partner with destiny, you can't believe the devil's lie because destiny doesn't lie. A lie is an intentional untruth made with deliberate intent to deceive. The moment you began to believe the devil's lie you've just eliminated God's plan for opportunity in your life. Jesus gives a clear description of the devil's character.

A lie is an intentional untruth made with deliberate intent to deceive.

"Ye are of your father the devil, and the lusts of your father ye will do. He was a murderer from the beginning, and abode not in the truth, because there is no truth in him. When he speaketh a lie, he speaketh of his own: for he is a liar, and the father of it," John 8:44. That description is full of red flags; Jesus was telling the disciples beware of who your father is because your actions will show whom you are truly serving. He also illuminates the nature of the devil. Liars cannot tell the truth; they have to lie to try to cover a lie. NEVER can the truth come forth from a habitual liar.

"He was a murderer from the beginning," helps us understand Satan's deception in the Garden of Eden when He deceived Eve into believing if she ate of the tree of knowledge of good and evil she would be as God. What she obviously didn't understand was that she was already made in His image. His murderous deceit caused man to die a natural and spiritual death. God sent His only begotten son Jesus to redeem man back to a righteous state. Because there was no truth in Satan, God expelled Him from heaven. The song of David said, *"He that telleth lies shall not tarry in my sight,"* Psalms 101:7. This certainly includes Satan. Jesus said, *"I beheld Satan as lighting fall from heaven,"* Luke 10:18. Don't allow the devil to detour your destiny and lie about your genealogy. *"But you are a chosen generation, a royal priesthood, a holy nation, a peculiar people,"* I Peter 2:9.

Every time you dare to believe, you put a demand on God. He says, finally, someone who believes me instead of Satan. The Father then dispatches angels, *"For he shall give his angels charge over thee, to keep thee in all thy ways,"* Psalm 91:11. Angels began to work on your behalf to help bring your destiny into fruition; it will begin to take form. Your planned efforts to bring your vision to past, continual seeking of God's plan for your life, and wisdom to know that your destiny doesn't encompass Satan's lie will open the gateway to fulfilled dreams, visions, and purpose. God has given you power over Satan, according to Luke 10:19. You have the power to totally reject what Satan offers you as "truth."

You have the power to totally reject what Satan offers you as "truth."

It is critical to know Satan's origin, His purpose, and how He plans to fulfill it. This is important because Satan is your enemy, and you cannot fight the enemy without historical background, present-day blueprints, and foreknowledge of future advances. *"Be sober, be vigilant; because your adversary the devil, as a roaring lion, walketh about, seeking whom he may devour," I Peter 5:8.* You must read God's historical blueprint (the Bible) to get this pertinent information. Also, through constant communication with your destiny partner (God) you will constantly receive updates of Satan's new strategies and how to combat them.

Satan's main objective as stated by Jesus is this, *"The thief cometh not, but for to steal, and to kill, and to destroy," John 10:10.* Jesus calls Him a thief; He comes to steal your dream, vision, and purpose. A thief is one who takes from you dishonestly and secretly without your knowledge. If Satan can get you to believe that the promises of God will never be fulfilled in your life, He has just gotten control of your faith and will end your story. Every time you believe what Satan is telling you about your destiny, you become the lie, you begin to partner with an untruth, and it opposes what God is telling you about your destiny.

"For I know the thoughts that I think toward you, said the Lord, thoughts of peace, and not of evil, to give you an expected end," Jeremiah 29:11. This is the truth about your destiny! If you dare to believe the truth about what God says about you, you'll be the lender and not the borrower, the head and not the tail, above only and not beneath and whatsoever you do shall prosper. Partner with destiny, and you'll be positioned to see God's plan fulfilled in your life.

CHAPTER EIGHTEEN

Positioned for Kingdom Connections

Ever heard of the saying "the right place at the right time"? Your destiny link is dependent upon being positioned, the right place or appropriate place. You can easily miss what God has for you if you fail to be in the right place. Placement is paramount because it ensures you are in the path of your destiny partner.

Placement is paramount because it ensures you are in the path of your destiny partner.

Take Hadassah, who was renamed Esther, for example. The book of Esther tells the story of her success, because she was positioned for kingdom connections. God is your direct link to people, resources, and plans for your fulfilled purpose on earth.

There was a king named Ahasuerus who reigned from India even unto Ethiopia over 127 provinces. The king made a feast during the third year of his reign of seven days and on the seventh day called for Queen Vashti to attend the feast, but she refused. At her refusal the princes asked what should be done unto the queen. They said she had not done wrong to the king only but to all the princes and the people in the provinces of King Ahasuerus.

The verdict, King Ahasuerus banished her. The princes said, *"If it please the king, let there go a royal commandment from him, and let it be written among the laws of the Persians and the Medes, that it be not altered, That Vashti come no more before king Ahasuerus; and let the king give her royal estate unto another that is better than she," Esther 1:19.* If Queen Vashti had known that Esther was (positioned) in Sushan, one of the 127 provinces ruled by the king, and that she would be exiled, she probably would have come when asked by the king.

Your neglect to use your God-given power to bring glory to His kingdom will cause you to lose your position to another. It was four years before the king could enjoy a suitable replacement, a fair young virgin, Esther. Don't lose patience when God is partnering you with destiny. The king had the power to rule and govern within his provinces, and he did so during his twenty-one-year reign, choosing to seek out a destiny partner that was well fit.

Don't lose patience when God is partnering you with destiny.

Mordecai raised Esther (a Jew), his uncle's daughter, and he instructed her not to reveal her ethnic background to the king (a Gentile). Timing is everything. In some cases revealing your identity prematurely may cause abortion of your connection. Make sure you are in the timing of God. Don't allow excitement overrule your judgment in the destiny connection.

Esther was selected among many for purification with oil of myrrh for six months and sweet odors for six months. When God is positioning you to rule and govern dominions and kingdoms, you must be prepared—it is critical. Don't wait until opportunity knocks and then try to prepare; it won't work. Following shows what happened when Esther was obedient to God, Mordecai, and Hegai, the keeper of the women. *"So Esther was taken unto king Ahasuerus into his house royal in the tenth month, which is the month of Tebeth, in the seventh year of his reign," Esther 2:16.* She was immediately given authority that she did not have just one year prior because of her obedience and preparation.

The power of obedience to God's order caused her to be in a wealthy place. When God brings you to that place remember, *"But thou shalt remember the Lord thy God: for it is he that giveth thee power to get wealth," Deuteronomy 8:18.* Esther remembered the Lord her God and acknowledged that His hand brought her to a place of great wealth. DON'T forget GOD when He brings you out of the state of mediocrity into a place of destiny.

DON'T forget GOD when He brings you out of the state of mediocrity into a place of destiny.

The king reigned twenty-one years. He chose Esther (because of God's hand) to become queen during his seventh year on the throne; that means Esther was queen over 127 provinces for fourteen years. God has a specific time and place of where He wants you to be in the kingdom and in your life. It is imperative that you follow His exact plan in order not to miss it.

Esther 3 and 4 unfolds the sinister plot by the king's right-hand man, Haman, to destroy all the Jews. Mordecai would not pay homage to Haman, and he was wroth. As a result he went before the king and told him, there are people scattered aboard and are different from all the people in the provinces of the kingdom; they do not keep his laws, and it would not profit the king to spare them.

Unbeknown to the king, Haman was plotting deceit against Queen Esther, her people, and the kingdom at large. Know them that labor among you to ensure that they are the chosen vessels that God wants to be a part of your destiny. The king therefore told Haman to do what seemed good in the best interest of the kingdom. When Mordecai perceived what was to be done unto the Jews he rent his clothes, put on sackcloth with ashes, went out in the midst of the city, and cried with a loud and bitter cry. Haman's plan entailed that on the thirteenth day, of the twelfth month, the Jews would be destroyed.

It was time for Queen Esther to use her position that God had placed her in to save her people. God is in the people business. Kingdom connections are purposed by God to bring Him ultimate glory, not for selfish gain or filthy lucre. *"When the righteous are authority, the people rejoice," Proverbs 29:2.* You may be in position to save your family, neighborhood, community, city, state, nation, and the world through innovative ideas, technological advancement, wealthy positions of authority, and the gift of healing or mere words spoken. But you will never know until you exercise your authority of faith in the position God has strategically placed you in.

God is in the people business.

Esther explained to Mordecai that the law said if anyone man or woman came into the king's presence without an invitation from the king he or she would be killed. This is what Mordecai conveyed to Esther in the fourth chapter. *"Then Mordecai commanded to answer Esther, Think not with thyself that thou shalt escape in the king's house, more than all the Jews," verse 13.* He further validates his claim. *"For if thou altogether holdest thy peace at this time, then shall there enlargement and deliverance arise to the Jews from another place; but thou and thy father's house shall be destroyed: and who knoweth whether thou art come to the kingdom for such a time as this?" verse 14.*

Mordecai said don't think selfishly; God has chosen you to approach the king on our behalf. She said, *"I will go in unto the king, which is not according to the law: and if I perish, I perish," Esther 4:16.* Esther was willing to die for what she believed was right. She dared to believe the words of Mordecai for the saving of her people. You must take a firm stand and know that God's arrow of deliverance is near. Esther, her maidens, and all the Jews immediately went on a three-day fast to seek God for mercy and deliverance. She realized her position was orchestrated by God to fulfill His plan for His people.

She dared to believe God would lift up a standard against the enemy, and she partnered with believers through fasting to break the yokes of Satan. On the third day, she prepared a banquet for the king and Haman, and as she went before the king, she found favor in his sight. The king asked Esther what was her request and her petition would be granted even half of the kingdom. Do you not know that the earth is the Lord's, and everything and everybody belongs to Him? *"The king's heart is in the hand of the Lord, as the rivers of water: he turneth it whithersoever he will," Proverbs 21:1.* Queen Esther now had the king's ear because God had turned his heart toward her.

Esther again had another banquet, and the king and Haman attended. It was then that Esther unveiled Haman's plot to destroy all the Jews. King Ahasuerus was wroth and granted the Jews the right to defend themselves and destroy their enemies. Restitution was rewarded, *"So they hanged Haman on the gallows that he had prepared for Mordecai. Then was the king's wrath pacified," Esther 7:10.* Your kingdom connection may be to deliver a nation—you never know. If the power is in your hand to deliver, do it.

The narrative of Esther's rise from an unnoticed Jewish girl to queen of a powerful empire depicts how God uses events and people to fulfill His promise to His chosen elect. *"But ye are a chosen generation, a royal priesthood, a holy nation, a peculiar people; that ye should show forth the praises of him who hath called you out of darkness into his marvelous light," I Peter 2:9.* God is bringing you out of some dark situations so that you to can partner with destiny. Your royal state as a vessel of the Almighty God merits you the benefits of kingdom-driven connections. Now, look into your destiny with the promise and dare to believe that God will never forsake you.

CHAPTER NINETEEN

Just Wait and See

Has someone, your parents maybe, close friend, ever told you, "just wait and see"? The waiting part was the most difficult I'm sure because you wanted to see the manifestation sooner than later.

When you partner with destiny, there is a waiting process, and you will see the rewards of not hurrying the plan of God for your life. Waiting does not mean standing idle while time passes or hoping for luck to show up. Waiting is serving God and allowing the unfolding of His ultimate plan to continue to be the perpetual ideal that brings you gratification. It is with this thought that you dare to believe. With God as your destiny partner, your timing will never be off.

Esther, for example, had to go through the waiting process to be chosen among the fair young virgins, and after she was chosen, she still had to wait during her year-long purification process. It was not an instant magical formula that caused her to become Queen Esther.

The "waiting" was in her "seeing" herself as the destiny partner God had chosen for King Ahasuerus. She also had to wait for the perfect timing to unveil Haman's wicked plot against her people to the king. As a result of her waiting, she was able to see her people spared from the evils that were to wipe them out completely.

You see "waiting and seeing" is not a bad thing; it's part of God's life plan for you. Timing is everything, and waiting takes time.

Time was instituted by God for mankind, and it can be your friend if you allow it. Time helps you see what is needful gain or wasteful want. Sometimes God will put you in a position of waiting as to develop a closer walk with Him and help you avoid major oops. Waiting for the perfect timing of God will render sure results of success. Your outcome will be far more rewarding if you wait and see instead of rushing to see.

Time helps you see what is needful gain or wasteful want.

Look at God the Creator when He decided to strategically map out this world, which is full of beauty, in Genesis the first chapter. God chose to take six days to speak, form, and create His ultimate masterpiece, which He could have done in one day. Why hurry perfection? God does not move haphazardly; He moves with intention, purpose, and manifestation. Everything that God spoke, Genesis records, *"God saw that it was good."* God charted out His plan of destiny for mankind and waited to see the manifestation of His glory. Note: He *rested* on the seventh day. Resting from your work *is* part of God's ultimate life plan for you as well.

The first day God separated light from darkness. On the second day, He made heaven and divided the waters from the heaven. The third day He called forth the sea, land, and vegetation. On the fourth day God said let there be celestial bodies, the sun, moon, and stars. The fifth day God spoke animal life of the sea and air. On the sixth day God called forth animal life on the earth. Also on the sixth day, *"God created man in his own image, in the image of God created he him; male and female created he them," Genesis 1:27*, climaxing all that He had accomplished. We were the ultimate creation. God could have chosen to speak everything into existence and left the earth as it was. But because He loved us so much, He chose to take the time to form mankind and see the results of His handiwork.

"And the Lord God formed man of the dust of the ground, and breathed into his nostrils the breath of life; and man became a living soul," Genesis 2:7. He didn't stop there! *"And the Lord God caused a deep sleep to fall upon Adam, and he slept: and he took one of his ribs, and closed up the flesh instead thereof; And the rib, which the Lord God had taken from man, made he a woman, and brought her unto the man," Genesis 2:21–22.* God took the necessary time to bring into fruition the image in His mind. God has put some detailed images in your mind about His ultimate plan for your destiny. Don't get discouraged because you don't see it right away.

Waiting to see the glory of God revealed in your life is worth it. The time it takes to hurry will cost you more time than it will to see the fruit of your patience. *"But let patience have her perfect work, that ye may be perfect and entire, wanted nothing," James 1:4 .* When God speaks destiny into your spirit, it's your guarantee. *"So shall my word be that goeth forth out of my mouth: it shall not return unto me void, but it shall accomplish that which I please, and it shall prosper in the thing whereto I sent it," Isaiah 55:11.*

Abram was promised a son by God and that his seed would be mighty upon the earth, in Genesis 15. Daring to believe God seemed difficult because he and his wife were of an old age. At the time of God's promise to Abram, he was ninety-nine years old and Sarah ninety. Instead of waiting on God, Abram had an alternate plan in that he slept with Hagar, Sarai's handmaid, at Sarai's suggestion and produced Ishmael. They both still had to wait and see God keep His promise to them despite their detour.

In the process of time God changed their names to Abraham (father of a multitude) and Sarah (princess, mother of nations). God changed their names making a covenant with Abraham saying, *"thou shalt be a father of many nations."* Afterward, He used Abraham to save Lot and his family from the destruction of Sodom and Gomorrah. Then Sarah bore Isaac unto them at the time He had appointed Abraham then being a hundred years old.

Because of Abraham and Sarah's doubt, they *disturbed* the plan of God for their destiny. The moral of the story is "Just wait and see." Don't go against the grain when God's word has been spoken concerning your destiny. God doesn't make mistakes and He cannot lie. *"God is not a man, that he should lie; neither the son of man, that he should repent: hath he said, and shall he not do it? Or hath he spoken, and shall he not make it good?" Numbers 23:19.*

If you don't believe the devil's lie and are positioned for kingdom connections, you will see the manifestation of your waiting. *"Eye hath not seen, nor ear heard, neither have entered into the heart of man, the things which God hath prepared for them that love him," I Corinthians 2:9.*

LIFE APPLICATION

1. God should be your prime destiny partner. He knows what investments you should make both naturally and spiritually. He has the perfect timing for your destiny. And He will never lead you in the wrong direction concerning His promise for your life. Who is your destiny partner?

2. Satan was a liar from the beginning. He will always lie about your destiny. Everything He says about your salvation, health, wealth, and relationships is a lie. Who will you believe? God or Satan?

3. God has already chosen who and what your kingdom connections should be. Don't take detours thinking that you have everything figured out. Will you be lead by God concerning the people He wants to connect you to and the position He wants to put you in?

4. Don't be in a rush to delve into something that's not part of your destiny. God has perfect timing. You will

not miss what God has for you if you are willing to acknowledge Him as your ultimate destiny partner. Are you willing to wait and see what God has ahead for you?

EPILOGUE

The Story Behind "Dare to Believe"

❧

"Forasmuch as ye are manifestly declared to be the epistle of Christ minis-tered by us, written not with ink, but with the Spirit of the living God; not in tables of stone, but in fleshy tables of the heart."
2 CORINTHIANS 3:3

I'm going to be extremely transparent in hopes that someone will have the courage and strength to breakthrough any remaining strongholds and fears. I pray that you dare to believe God for the impossible.

I grew up believing God for anything. I mean anything. From birth through age five are a child's formidable years; from that time onward I was taught to believe consistently. I believed kindergarten was going to be full of fun and nothing was impossible. It was then that my parents taught me "God can do anything but fail." I believed my parents loved me; they taught me the difference between right and wrong, success and failure, and fear and belief. My father was a pastor for forty-three years teaching faith and living by faith, my mother likewise. I believed it and tested it.

If I woke up with a headache I'd pray and ask God to heal me. When I had problems at school, I'd pray and ask God to solve them and He did. When I needed or even wanted something I had faith to believe God would provide it for me. It seemed that my prayers worked almost every time. I thought, "Wow, what an incredible power to have to be able to talk to an Unseen Power and get an answer." This seemed to be a phenomenon; I realized it was inherent, which to me was overwhelming.

As I grew older, I became doubtful and tried to work things out on my own. Bad mistake! Fear began to grip me taking me on a detour, and I could no longer hear God. I woke up one day to so many unsolved problems, bad decisions, and a world of mixed messages about faith. It took God to restore what my parents had planted, daring faith.

CHAPTER TWENTY

Exploring How Faith Works

I had to further explore *how* this thing called faith worked for myself. I would hear my father say, "faith without works is dead." What did Daddy mean I thought? You can have faith, but if you don't do anything with it, it is idle. Throughout grade school I believed I could make the grade, remember the speech, and do my best at being the best me. Yes, I had external challenges and internal wars that would buffet me time after time, but I knew greater was on the inside. As I grew older and transitioned into my high schools years, different challenges came—passing college preparatory tests, learning a foreign language, peer pressure, and trying to understand teenagers who thought the world revolved around them.

I knew that out of nine hundred high school freshmen, it was going to take consistent application and mental and moral perseverance to prove I was worthy at the end of a four-year journey to walk across the stage and earn my diploma. Although I had many bumps and bruises during my course, I stuck with it and became salutatorian. I was proud that at the end I was one of the four hundred out of the nine hundred who started that graduated. Many will start with you, but few will end with you.

My faith was becoming increasingly stronger and I believed. I believed. With diligence and persistence I was accepted to one of the top ten universities in the nation. And at the end, you have to know that you know that God has handpicked you to go further and do more. Even as Paul encouraged the church at Philippi in Philippians 3:14, no matter how tough it becomes *"press toward the mark"* or the goal you've set for yourself.

I was taught faith and therefore learned to practice it. I guess it was the "practice what you preach" that pushed me to a place of pure belief in God. By the time I'd reached college, DARE to Believe was ingrained in the fabric of my spirit and soul. I'd regained my confidence in God again. I couldn't help but believe that with Jesus Christ as my nucleus that all things were possible.

I'd seen all eight of my older siblings attend college and become successful. Why was I any different? They had set the bar, and I knew with technological advancement I was expected to excel. Talking about a challenge, this certainly was one that took every ounce of courage I had. I almost threw in the towel during my last semester, but God wouldn't let me quit. As a result of my faith in the Almighty God, I earned a B.S. in journalism—news editorial. He knew one day He'd tell me to write this book and others, and a degree in writing would certainly support those efforts.

God knows the path you will take. It may seem that detours keep surfacing in your life, but as a witness, if you put your faith in God

He will lead you down the right path of success. I explored other avenues that I *thought* would get me to an expected end, but I ended up going in circles trying to find faith in people, things, and abstract notions. I woke up one day and realized God was there waiting for my exploration to end. He embraced me with open arms and showed me exactly what faith really meant.

CHAPTER TWENTY-ONE

My Faith Challenged

After college I went on a tour of life that I'd not intended. I'd become what I call a "statistic of faith." All my life I was taught faith, experienced faith, and encouraged others to have faith. But when my "real" turn came, I was just like all the other people I'd seen over the years, running from the face of God, because I didn't know how to stand firm and dare to believe He would deliver.

Well, I had enough of Satan's venom and I needed antivenom to cure my bite of doubt. This bite was deadly, and if God didn't send help fast, I was going to be walking dead. I needed an antidote that was so potent that it would last the rest of my life. It came and was injected right into the chambers of my heart (place of decision making).

I told you in the introduction that God sent me to Portland, Oregon, in August of '07 for ministry, and I had to believe Him on a totally different level. I'd never taught Sunday School, Bible study, YPWW (young people willing workers), or any form of preaching the Gospel, so this was absolutely ludicrous to me. After a couple of months warring back and forth with God, I was obedient.

Not even a month in the city, I was asked to preach at a church! Preach, I thought! "You have the wrong sister," I told the church administrator. "I don't preach." "I have a sister that can really, really preach." So I thought she was mistaken. I accepted the ministry engagement upon her insistence that she said God told her ME. God moved mightily in that service, and I thought, "Whew, now that that's over, I'm good." God was saying full-time ministry, and I was saying this is not God! I said, "God, I've been obedient and moved— now this is something totally different." Instead of heeding the call to ministry, I underwent seventeen interviews and was denied employment. I couldn't believe it—no one would hire me! I had no other choice but to trust God. He will leave you without options so that you can say YES to His will and plan for your life. It was then that I dared to believe God concerning His word that He'd planted in me as a young child.

I had no other choice but to trust God.

I use to write down scriptures for my father in spiral notebooks, note I said notebooks with an *s*. I wondered why Daddy didn't just read straight from the Bible when he got ready to preach. I mean, he had me writing scripture after scripture! What I didn't realize was God was instilling faith in me then and preparing me for what was to come. I cannot tell you how many revival crusades, miracles of healing and deliverance, new territory, testimonies of victory, concerts, and other venues God has blessed me to experience because He challenged my faith by me accepting the external dare. What is God challenging you to do? Will you answer the call? Trust me it's easier to say yes than it is taking the scenic route!

CHAPTER TWENTY-TWO

Operating in Faith

It was November of '07 when I was in revival, three months to the day that I'd relocated; my "icon of faith" made his eternal transition, my Daddy. I thought, "God, this cannot be so." Every trail and challenge I had ever gone through had become relevant.

I finished the revival and headed to Chicago to raise my father from the dead. Yes, I said command life into a dead body! I had just come off a thirty-one-day fast in October in preparation for miracles that would take place in the revival. God said to me, "Do you believe I'm able to do it?" I responded, "Yes, I believe." God said, "It is absolutely critical that you follow my exact instructions." When God speaks He doesn't waste words. He told me to go on a three day and night fast. I didn't even tell my family what I was believing God for. Sometimes you have to keep what God has shared with you until the right timing. At the word of God, I fasted for three days and nights not knowing that I would have to help drive from Oregon to Illinois, a 2200 mile journey.

When you are obedient to the Father, He will show you His great wonders. Upon arriving to Chicago after thirty-eight hours, I got some needed rest and headed to the funeral home with my sister Vanessa and our family friend Vanessa. My soul was connected to God, and I could clearly hear Him. It had been five days that my father was deceased. While waiting see to my father, I shared with Vanessa, the family friend, how God was saying, "Dare to Believe." She said, "Evelyn, you have persuaded me also. I'm going in the room with you." Now both of us had seen with our own eyes a few years earlier my father come out of a coma at the word of God. So our faith in God had already been proven. It's imperative that you don't share what God has spoken to you about your destiny with doubtful people; they will cause you to detour. Connect with a true believer.

My soul was connected to God, and I could clearly hear Him.

As we waited and waited, my faith grew stronger and stronger. The mortician said, "He's not ready yet. We have not prepped him for viewing. Can you come back tomorrow?" I said, "I don't mean any harm, but I've driven 2200 miles to see my father." Now, no one but my friend (Vanessa) and my sister Vanessa knew why I wanted to see my Dad. The morticians said, "Okay, give us a few minutes." As we were waiting I heard, God say, "Don't be afraid of what you see." I told you your eyes are the sense that we believe beyond all others. I had to use my spiritual sight, dare to believe God, and operate in the invisible realm.

We entered the cold and unwelcoming room where he lay and began to speak the word of God over him. He was on a steel table with a white sheet over him, his hair grey, almost white and skin tone a smoky black. As we began to pray the prayer of faith, GOD heard us. We witnessed something we never had seen in our entire lives.

God said to me, "Anoint his head with oil," and I did. He said, "Blow on him." I did. As I began to blow on him, his pigmentation began to come back, and the darkness began to leave. God said, "Blow on him again," and I did. I was in utter shock. I said to Vanessa, "Do you see what I see?" She screamed yes! We began to pray louder and more fervently. As we prayed our faith increased and God showed us more signs of how real He was. I began to anoint his feet, legs, and his chest. His feet were moveable and warm. Vanessa came over, touched his feet, and screamed again.

Everything Daddy had taught me was coming to life! I couldn't doubt God anymore; I had seen Him in full operation. We prayed so loud until they put us out of the funeral home. They said we were disturbing other families that were in mourning. As we left I asked the mortician when do they usually embalm the body; he said as soon as they pick up the body. Now correct me if I'm wrong, but embalming fluid doesn't move.

We returned to the car sharing with my sister Vanessa what we had just witnessed. She cried, and cried; we cried and cried. I said to my friend Vanessa, "I have to ask you one question. "Did you see my Daddy's chest move?" She screamed, let go of the steering wheel in the middle of the street, and said, "Yes, we let them put us out too soon!" I say to you, don't let *anyone* stop, cut off, or impede what God has designed to be your blessing, birthright, or miracle.

I'm including this passage of my life to encourage you to believe beyond the realm of impossibilities. I cannot tell you how much this notable miracle of God has impacted my faith walk.

As we attended the home going services, Friday night and Saturday morning God continued to show us and others how mighty He is. Friday night as I walked down the long aisle of the processional viewing, the last one in the line, I again prayed over my father and asked that God raise him from the dead, letting out a loud bitter cry. During the service I shared with the congregation what happened at the funeral home, some people were in utter disbelief, others amazed at the glory of God, and many waiting for him to get up out of the casket.

See, my father was known as God's Miracle Man of Faith and Power. People came from near and far to Kneeway (the name of my father's church) expecting a miracle, expecting God to heal them. Our church was a hospital of faith, a healing center. My father put up tents and held revivals from the Midwest to the Southern coast. People were saved, healed, delivered, and set free. He was one that would fast for days on in.

As a result, God wrought many miracles by his hand. A lady named Amie Chandler attended Kneeway who had uterine cancer and was bleeding constantly. The doctors told her she would never have children, and they "wouldn't take a nickel for her life." Her skin was thin as paper, and her time was running out. As my father entered her house to pray for her, she said she felt a powerful wind come in with him. He asked if she believed God would heal her and she said yes. He prayed the prayer of faith for her, and immediately her issue dried up. God had healed her. Thereafter, she had six children.

There was another woman who grew up in my father's church who was in a car accident. She was seven months pregnant and was experiencing trauma as a result of the accident. Her sisters said to her, "Faye, you are starting to stink." She went to the doctor and found out her baby was dead. They told her she needed immediate surgery to remove the baby or else she would die to. She said, "Let me go get prayer from my pastor, and if God doesn't raise my baby then I'll let you do surgery." She came to Kneeway, and my father laid his hands on her stomach and prayed the prayer of faith. As she returned to her seat, the baby started kicking! She screamed with joy and excitement. Two months later completing the pregnancy term delivered a healthy baby boy, Earl.

Another woman came to Bible study one Wednesday night with a blind seeing cane. As she maneuvered to the front of the church, she asked if my father remembered her. He said no. She said I'm sister such and such. She said she used to come under the tent revivals years ago. He asked what happened to her sight, and she said she had gone blind from diabetes. He laid his hands on her eyes and again prayed the prayer of faith. One of the elders assisted her back to her seat. When she'd almost reached her seat, she screamed, "I can see. I can see." I was awestruck. A miracle right before my very eyes! Opening of the blind eyes were miracles I had read about in the Bible. This faith module so to speak was really working.

These are only three of the multiplicity of notable miracles that God performed over the forty-three years of my father's ministry.

I was born right in the midst of this great faith walk thrusting me to a place of pure belief in God. By the time my twin and I arrived on the seen, my father had already been in the faith walk for over a decade. He had found his niche, his calling, and chose to remain faithful until the day he made his eternal transition. This is why I've called him my "icon of faith." There should be someone in your life your circle of influence that has caused you to operate in unstoppable faith. If there is not, that means your circle is too small. Don't be afraid to expand your horizons.

As we were concluding the funeral services for my father, God continued to show Himself strong. Saturday morning we arrived for the second home going service, and as the morticians open the casket, my father's head was turned toward the congregation! Those who had come on Friday night and saw him facing the ceiling began to mutter to one another, "How did this happen?" I'll tell you—faith mixed with an incredible act of God!

I'm sure by now as a reader you wondering how much of this is true, all of it. God is saying, "Dare to believe me, I breathed on Adam the first man and I can breathe life again into whom I will." Many have read about Elisha raising the Shunammite woman's son in 2 Kings 4, Jesus raising Lazarus in John 11, and Peter raising Dorcas in Acts 10, why should now be any different from then? God has not changed. He's the same today, yesterday, and forever more. According to your faith be it unto you. Operate in faith without fear. God will not let you down. He told Jeremiah shall not one word that you speak fail thee, as long as you are in my will.

CHAPTER TWENTY-THREE

Trails Come to Make You

My life was altered forever after the death of my father. While He did not get up physically, he continues to live through the faith of his seed. I believe God has given me his spiritual mantle. I carry it with honor and believe that one day God will use me to raise the physical dead. I now operate in faith with no reservations. God has used me to speak life to many dead situations. I dare to believe God to conquer external challenges while releasing internal faith to partner with the predestined plans of Him who created me.

I realized my father has left a legacy that will never die. "Dare to believe" God for the miraculous will be passed on from generation to generation. He had faith to perform miracles and to inherit eternal life with God the Father. Paul said to be absent from the body is to be present with the Lord. I believe if you serve God with all your heart while you are in your earthen vessel, your trials will not be compared to the things God has in store for you.

I faced many trails thereafter, causing my faith to stretch and grow. The stretching hurt and the growing didn't feel so great either. I had to develop a more intimate relationship with God when my father passed. He was the nucleus that held my spiritual walk in place. I needed to know where to filter my experiences and mature my relationship with God. I sought God in February of 2009 through a ten day consecrated fast birthing this book "DARE to Believe." I could barely hear God's voice as it was weakening beneath the woes of life. Here I was in a new city, with a new calling and new gifts. I cried out to God and asked what He was saying about my life and the challenges I was facing.

On this ten-day consecration, God revealed to me that my trials only came to make me. I thought, "Couldn't you have found another way, God?" But the only way that I truly sought Him with my whole heart was through my trials. I couldn't lean to the arms of flesh because they were too weak to uphold and sustain my weight. The weight of life was leaving me lifeless, and I needed a lifeline of unwavering faith. I trusted Him through every trial: spiritual, social, economic, and physical.

I came to a pivotal point in my life when I journeyed to Africa in August of 2009 for three weeks on a mission trip; my faith was being stretched. My journey to Africa began way before I even stepped foot on African soil. Through the support of many, I was able to raise the money needed through three fundraiser concerts and several revival crusades. I had to believe that God was sending me and that He would make provision for me. It was my first time out of the United States and how wonderful it was to carry to gospel to other nations.

Tears began to flow down my cheeks as I made my final connection from Seattle, WA, to Portland, OR, journeying home from Africa. I realized how blessed I was to have clean drinking water, hot water to bathe, electricity, a flushing toilet, modern shelter, and plenty of food at my disposal. My trials seemed to weaken beneath the woes of those who were less fortunate than I.

Despite the lack of technological advancement in many areas, the praise, worship, and prayer in Rwanda, Burundi, and Kenya were unprecedented. Our brothers and sisters in these nations truly serve God without limits. My heart rejoiced with them as we saw God bring healing, perform miracles, and bestow joy to many. God graced me to meet President Barak Obama's grandmother, what an honor. My vision, dreams, and plans God had given me came into focus when I reached beyond natural limits without breaking, when I stretched my faith.

Because of my obedience and willingness to sacrifice my time, money, body, and spiritual preparation, my reward was great: my faith catapulted to another dimension. I returned to the United States with a new appreciation of my relationship with God. I again journeyed overseas to Italy in 2011 giving way to new horizons. Taking the gospel through song to Europe broadened my perspective on daring to believe the global God that He is. The outdoor evangelical festival served as a medium to and for so many souls to receive Jesus Christ. Now I have access to a world of opportunity to spread the gospel of Jesus Christ using my faith without limits. You can too.

Don't allow fear and the trails of life hold you captive. Your trails come to make you.

I dare you (external dare) to ignite your faith (internal dare) that God has given you to make your dream and vision a reality. Unlock and unleash your faith to help make a better you and leave your legacy in the earth realm. Dare to Believe!

LIFE APPLICATION

1. Each of us has a story; we are living epistles. Your story is important. Are you willing to unveil and share it in order to help others believe? Think of a venue or platform where you can share your experience that will enhance the lives of others. Becoming transparent during and after your faith walk, trials, and triumphs will strengthen you.

2. How has life experience helped you build a closer walk with God?

3. Your faith should be used in every area of your life: spiritually, mentally, socially, and financially. See yourself as an entrepreneur, creating ideas that will cause you to live by the tree of life perpetually, building the kingdom becoming a historical marker. Are you willing to stretch your faith?

4. Dare to believe. Is there something you've read in this book relative to where you are in your destiny walk? Did a word, phrase, or sentence remind you of what God has told you about your destiny?

CONCLUSION

From infancy to adulthood we learn how to utilize our inborn faith. It is no wonder that we matriculate from faith to faith and from glory to glory. Our faith is constantly maturing as our relationship with God develops. By faith we are able to perform major self inabilities such as breathing. We inhale and exhale without taking conscious notation unless it is inhabited by an external or internal force.

External challenges come in three forms: God, Satan, and human will. God will cause external turbulence to buffet you to push you into your destiny. Challenges brought on by Satanic solicitations and human will are allowed by God causing you to stretch your faith. The enemy is not self-created; therefore He must gain permission from God to test your faith. The external dare enacted by human will is prompted to challenge you to go beyond what others believe you are incapable of performing. The courage to prove otherwise takes the mental and moral strength to persevere beyond fear or difficulty.

Utilizing this internal faith given to every human by God will ultimately strengthen your belief in Him, catapult your destined purpose to another realm, and cause others to believe in God as they see you triumph. The courage to do so will yield countless victories and rewards.

Your faith is not predicated on how much you have, just your utilization of it. As you use the mustard seed of faith that God has dealt to you, faith naturally expands and rises to the occasion. The occasion may be on behalf of another or yourself for healing (emotional, mental, or financial), prosperity, or salvation. You must nourish your faith daily through the word of God by reading what is already in print. With every step of faith, God is there to guide you through every challenge as with the parent who guides the child while learning how to walk.

Throughout your walk of faith, it is suggested that you choose God as your ultimate destiny partner. He will be there when no one else will. He said, *"I will never leave thee, nor forsake thee," Hebrew 13:5.* Every dream you dare to come true will manifest as long as you don't believe the devil's lie. The moment you trade the truth about your destiny for Satan's lie, you forfeit God's personal promise for your obedience: *"The Lord shall open unto thee his good treasure, the heaven to give the rain unto thy land in his season, and to bless all the work of thine hand: and thou shalt lend unto many nations, and thou shalt not borrow," Deuteronomy 28:12.*

You have been positioned for kingdom connections in order that God may prosper you. Positioning is important when daring to believe because if you are not in the place where God wants you both naturally and spiritually, you will miss the fullness of your purpose. God created you on purpose, with a purpose, and for a purpose. You want to live a purposeful life, one full of repeated destiny. Your desire should be to embrace the complete will of God for your life mentally, spiritually, financially, socially, and physically.

God has packaged a life plan for you willing that you embrace, employ, explore, and expand every facet available to you through the utilization of your faith. Every goal, vision, and dream will come alive manifesting itself repeatedly because you dared to believe.

ACKNOWLEGMENTS

I want to express my personal and sincere thanks especially to:

God the Father—who gives me the breath I breathe daily to accomplish the assignments He has given me in the earth realm. You are the foundation of my existence. This book is founded upon your unrelenting perpetual word that never fails. Thank you God for creating me to *yield* what you established in me—FAITH. I DARE TO BELEIVE you for everything you've promised me. You keep pushing me to go beyond my scope, and I'm becoming a better me everyday. It was your unyielding love that kept me grounded. Thank you for not giving up on me.

Without God and the people He sends in our lives, we can't possibly accomplish minor or major goals. Writing this book was a major goal, and it took God's choice vessels of believers to help push me to another place of faith. My sincere gratitude I express to:

Ronald Woolfolk—former director of liberal arts and science (LAS) transition program at the University of Illinois at Champaign-Urbana. You convinced me that journalism was my niche and pushed me to believe in four years I could earn a degree in journalism news-editorial. Thank you, Ron, for truly believing in me when I didn't believe in myself.

Pastor Provine Turner, Jr.—You just don't know how many times I came to Teaching God's Word Faith Ministries and wanted to throw in the towel. Each and every time God used you to speak a word that was relative to my destiny. You encouraged me to press on in spite of the challenges and caused my soul to believe I was destined to succeed. Thank you.

Rev. Dr. W. G. Hardy, Jr.—You've inspire me from the heart. God has placed an enriching sound in your soul, and it rings beyond the earthly realm into the spirit realm causing many to believe. You dared me to reach beyond the American borders into the Motherland of Africa and overseas to Europe to see what opportunities God had waiting for me. Many thanks.

Pastor Willie McCoy, Jr.—I must acknowledge that you have been my injection of faith from a little girl. You have been my counselor, confidante, and friend. I remember receiving a text from you when I got back from Africa in September of '09 that brought me to tears. It read "Smiling! Gummy I will give you the support for whatever you need to make happen." "Everything will be just fine I promise you that! If you need my help, don't hesitate to let me know." By this time I was in boohoo tears! Thank you, Doc, and I love you from my heart.

These three pastors walked with me through the toughest time of my life. Thanks a million, as my father would say!

Made in the USA
Charleston, SC
08 August 2012